PRAISE FOR *GAM*

M000189058

Time to level up! Dr. Lindsay Portno[...] in your learning environment an [...] n00b or a pro, you'll gain a deeper appreciation for what happens in the mind when engaged in play . . . and she sprinkles in a few hacks, tips, and Easter eggs to encourage you to up your game.

—**Amber Coleman-Mortley**, director of social engagement, iCivics, podcaster, and blogger @MomOfAllCapes

Lindsay Portnoy's *Game On? Brain On!* is the best informed, most usable, and best-written book on games and learning we now have for educators, teachers, and parents.

—**James Paul Gee**, author of *What Video Games Have to Teach Us about Learning and Literacy*

In this book, Lindsay Portnoy brilliantly shows us why and how to bring play's power into classrooms through games. The lessons learned in games are limitless. Fun and learning coincide.

—**Peter Gray**, research professor of psychology at Boston College and author of *Free to Learn: Why Releasing the Instinct to Play Will Make Our Children Happier, More Self-Reliant, and Better Students for Life*

Game On? Brain On! is a tremendous resource for educators using games in the classroom, educators thinking about using games, and those who didn't even know they should be considering the importance of play and learning! Lindsay Portnoy does a wonderful job emphasizing the importance of play in learning and how we need to ensure that we are addressing equity in terms of play.

—**Steve Isaacs**, teacher, game design and development, Bernards Township Public Schools

An engaging and concise read on why we need more play in our lives, filled with vivid examples and useful advice for incorporating play into the classroom, home, and our whole world! *Game On? Brain On!* is guaranteed to make you feel good while learning about play—just like a great, fun game!

—**Dr. Kat (Karen) Schrier**, author of *Knowledge Games* and editor of *100 Games to Use in the Classroom & Beyond*

GAME ON? BRAIN ON!

GAME ON?
BRAIN ON!

The Surprising Relationship between
Play and Gray (Matter)

by Lindsay Portnoy, PhD

Game On? Brain On!: The Surprising Relationship between Play and Gray (Matter)
© 2020 Lindsay Portnoy

This book is available at special discounts when purchased in quantity for educational purposes or as premiums, promotions, or fundraisers. For inquiries and details, contact the publisher at books@daveburgessconsulting.com.

Published by Dave Burgess Consulting, Inc.
San Diego, CA
DaveBurgessConsulting.com

Library of Congress Control Number: 2020941683
Paperback ISBN: 978-1-951600-42-6
Ebook ISBN: 978-1-951600-43-3

Cover design by Michael Miller
Interior design by Liz Schreiter
Editing and production by Reading List Editorial: readinglisteditorial.com

This book is dedicated to Judah & Levi,
whose love is the ultimate dub.

CONTENTS

AUTHOR'S NOTE

Okay, let's play a game . . . Ready? Go!

> Think of a number between one and ten. *Got it?*
> Multiply your number by five. *Still with me?*
> Okay, now add twenty-five to the product. *Ready?*
> Divide your new number by five. *Stick with me now.*
> Subtract your original number from your new number.

Do you have your number? Was your number five?*

What if I told you that everyone playing will get the same answer as you?

How do you feel right now? Maybe you're curious or confused. Perhaps you're even intrigued? If you've played along instead of skipping over the game, we have one thing in common: interest. Loosely defined as a goal-directed behavior toward a desired outcome, games are far more than a way to pass the time.[1] As we'll see in the following chapters, well-crafted games spark interest, engagement, and creativity, and they demonstrate what has been discovered during decades of research in learning science.

* It's always five! In fact, when our oldest son was five and we first played this game with him, we had him convinced that the answer was always five because he was five and obviously his was the most magical age of all.

> ## How to Use the QR Codes
> To access bonus content throughout the book, simply launch the camera on your iOS device and hover over the QR codes, or launch the QR reader on your Android phone.

INTRODUCTION:

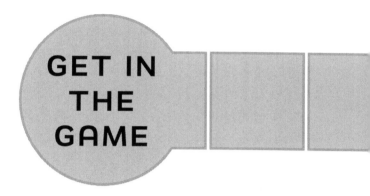

GET IN
THE
GAME

What travels faster than a Ferrari and carries over a quadrillion passengers?

Take a seat on one of the billion mighty neurons nested within the three-pound mass sitting between your ears, commonly known as your brain. The signals emitted from one neuron to another are called synapses, and they're traveling at a dizzying speed in excess of 270 miles per hour. These synapses are sending messages received by the dendrites of neighboring neurons and are the foundation of human thought. While the human brain makes up only 2 percent of the human body, it is the source of what makes us, us. It determines who we are, what we do, how we move, and how we think, act, and react to experiences in the world around us. The very attributes that make us, us are born in our brain.

Data gathered from a century of research in the science of learning, known as cognitive science, show that the use of different forms of engagement helps create optimal learning experiences. This research is enhanced by novel findings in neuroscience that show *how* we learn is as important as *what* we learn. Science, it turns out, is on the side of inherently playful learning! We are designed to learn by doing, through iteration and practice, alongside others.

THE SCIENCE OF LEARNING AND THE ART OF PLAY

What is the first game you remember playing as a child? Do you remember masking giggles behind the bathtub curtain while playing hide-and-seek with a sibling? Were you engaged in the relentless pursuit of the Easter egg in *Super Mario* that would bring you to the warp zone? Whether you were a pinball wizard or a winner at the Game of Life, game play was certainly an important part of your development.

Taking on roles, practicing new knowledge to develop a sense of competence and to gain autonomy in making choices, and doing so alongside others gives us purpose and a sense of relatedness as we gain, apply, and maintain skills. The games we play reveal not only how we learn best but also how we engage with the world. Paying attention to the games we, as educators, play and have played, as well as the games that our students engage with, allows us to reflect on the very nature of teaching and learning.

Throughout this book we'll unpack the games and playful experiences that invite engagement and deep learning. We'll look at the essential elements of games, from the rules of engagement, to the roles of players, to the different types of games, and we'll discuss the difference between gamification and game-based learning. We'll explore the many lessons that games have to teach, including collaboration, problem solving, critical thinking, perseverance, communication, empathy, and creativity. And together we'll delve into the research that explains why games provide an ideal template to not only understand but also to apply, synthesize, and create more impactful learning. We'll bust the assumptions of games for learning to discover that it's not *if* you play but *how* you play that matters most.

Like the Easter eggs hidden in our favorite childhood games, the QR codes you'll find throughout these pages will link to videos, tips, tools, and hidden surprises while you play along with your own learners! And because the power of play is often found in collaboration, the first QR code will take you straight to a study guide you can use with other educators as you level up through the pages. Game on!

WHO GETS TO PLAY?

Within the pages of this book are examples of how impactful play can be on our ability to grow, learn, and thrive in the world. In fact, I would argue that play is *the* most essential skill for learning about the world and preparing to take on the important and exciting decisions that determine our futures. However, what I've seen is that not everyone has the same access to play. My experience with play and education is vast. Growing up, I was a big gamer, which made me something of a rare duck at the time, as a female who was into games. As a tween, I spent many hours in front of my Nintendo intent on being the woman (playing as Mario or Luigi) who finally saved the princess. Perhaps I was saving myself? As I grew older, I discovered music and theater and learned that play could mean more than beating a Koopa Troopa in *Mario Bros.* But one of the critical aspects of game play remained: by taking on the roles of others in different times and space, I was given the opportunity to be the hero—at least for the moment.

Later, as a classroom teacher in the South Bronx, where I largely worked with Black and non-Black children of color whose parents loved them deeply but did not have access to the same tools and resources that my white, middle-class upbringing afforded, I quickly realized that not everyone had the same opportunity for play. With school systems increasingly focused on standardized tests, what chance there was for play was replaced with rote curriculums and "sit-and-get" instructional periods. As a result, I saw teachers getting physically ill and students in tears, wetting themselves, and developing anxiety as a result of the pressure to perform on assessments not made to see potential and provide supports, but rather to seek out deficits and enforce sanctions. With school funding tied to the results of these inequitable tests, schools like the one where I taught risked losing not only programs that fell outside of the core curriculum, but also staff members.

Seeing the inequity and hoping to understand and then help advocate to change it, I transitioned to a role as researcher. I also worked as a university professor at Hunter College, City University of New York, where I trained teachers working in classrooms across one of the largest public school districts in the country, which served both some of the most affluent and some of the most resource-deprived students in our country. At the same time, I became a parent, and as I navigated the city's schools, I saw firsthand the inequity baked into our current education system.

Beyond traditional education-related roles, I've also been an entrepreneur and founded an educational games company. In this role, I designed, developed, and play-tested games with students in the tristate area of New York, New Jersey, and Connecticut at schools, public spaces, museums, and libraries. In doing so, I spent time inside Title 1 public schools, where exhausted teachers tried to support far too many children in their classrooms with too few supports; public charter schools, where smaller classes of Black and non-Black students of color were trained to obediently SLANT (sit up, listen, ask and answer questions, and track the teacher visually) to show compliance; and suburban public and private schools, which served mostly white middle- and upper-class students. The contrasts in equity and access were stark, and the distinction in results, when one considered the resources and expectations of each school, were far from surprising.

Now I again find myself serving as a researcher and university professor, this time at Northeastern University in Boston. Though my roles have varied, along with the number of schools I work with and the students I encounter, what I have consistently observed is a very disturbing trend: the play gap continues to widen. Although the research—which we will explore in the following chapters—shows that play is an essential way to learn, it is immediately clear that there are affordances for those who already have and fewer affordances and far less flexibility for those who have less.

SYSTEMIC INEQUITIES IN ACCESS TO PLAY

How can we truly address the opportunity gap when it feels as if our systems are designed to work against and not for all our children, especially our students of color? Herein lies the complicated relationship between knowing one thing and doing something entirely different. More specifically, this is where we enter into a very pointed conversation about what it really means to have the keys to the playground and, later, the boardroom.

We're all familiar with the age-old depiction of equity, which involves three almost identical images with one small shift in each successive picture. In all three images, three children of varying heights attempt to peer over the fence and watch a baseball game in play. In the first image, only the tallest child can actually see the game. This image is called *injustice*.

In the second image, the same three children attempt to see over the fence, this time with all three standing on the same number of milk crates. Again, the tallest among them has the most expansive view, but this time, at least the others get a glimpse. This image is called *equality*, where everyone gets what's equal or the same. The last image includes all three children standing on a different number of milk crates, the number needed for each child to have a full view of the game in play. This image is called *equity* because everyone finally gets what they need. While I adore this image, I would present a fourth frame, one where there is no fence at all, and all children can comfortably see the game just as they are. This frame would be called *justice*.

It's interesting to stop and think about how often our children call attention to things they perceive to be unfair, whether that is one child receiving more help with their math homework at home or who is chosen at school to deliver the attendance to the office, a coveted task. The common refrain I would share with both my students and later my children is, "Fair doesn't mean everyone gets the same thing; it means everyone gets what they need."

In my classroom, I had a child who regularly complained about not being chosen to deliver the attendance. Though he very much wanted this honor, this child was a struggling reader whom school had mandated attend a remedial reading program and, beyond that, had mandated that the program be held at the same time each morning—exactly when attendance was due. Instead of getting to share in this coveted task, this child had to sit through another one of many poorly designed and, frankly, inequitable reading programs forced on our nation's most vulnerable populations, largely our most under-resourced populations of primarily Black and non-Black children of color.

This is where we falter as a society: when we don't see play for the opportunity it provides for learning and, moreover, when we don't provide the same affordances to all children. Systemic inequities don't allow all humans to experience play in the same way—at least not at the same time and in the same way and with the same materials. The schools where curriculum is rote and focused on the next standardized assessment are those serving traditionally low-resourced communities, which is code for Black and non-Black communities of color. It's ironic, then, that the things we're trying to demand by brute force through a sit-and-get curriculum are the very skills acquired through open-ended and thoughtful play. In our schools, our homes, and our society at large, there is an important conversation to be had about what it means to ensure everyone has access to the resources and skills they need to thrive. The difference between getting the same and getting what you need is what equity is all about.

This needs gap is also the root of inequities in our homes, in our classrooms, in our communities, in our world. The systems at play in our world are not set up to invite equity into each day at school, much less each night at home, where millions of children struggle with schoolwork with little to no support because caregivers must work multiple jobs to ensure basic care. I say *caregivers* intentionally here, as many of our nation's youth live with one parent, grandparents, other relatives, or care providers other than what our traditional verbiage of *parents* affords.

If, however, we make a slight pivot in our own perception, we might challenge our assumptions of sameness as ideal and instead look at differences as needs-based. Once we see the different needs of our students as opportunities to learn, we can take an asset-based approach that also allows us to see the rich attributes of each of our learners. This is in stark contrast to the current deficit-based approach, where nonlinear means noncompliant, and noncompliant means underfunded, and underfunded means no resources, and around and around we go. It's dizzying, yes?

What I'll offer in the following chapters is an alternative. You'll find countless examples of foundational knowledge acquired through a more authentic, empowering, and natural way of learning: play. These are not digital worksheets repurposed as the same "drill-and-kill" technique currently in use in classrooms across the globe. Instead, this is the intentional and flexible application of play to the learning that we know to be foundational to success.

Sure, math and science and literacy and history are embedded in the play you'll see in the following chapters. And there are also ways to formatively assess and concretely demonstrate the exponential learning that takes place in each dynamic space. But there are also lessons on navigating conflict when it arises and learning how to clearly communicate your thoughts. There's also the importance of shifting your beliefs when you know better. As Maya Angelou famously said, "When you know better, do better."

As we'll see in this book, the research is clear: we're born to play. And if we're intentional in our shared work, we can work to create equitable access to these playful experiences for all children. Perhaps it's time we take a note from Dr. Angelou and do just that.

Choose Your Own Journey?

While the following pages point to the countless ways we can make learning visible while actually having fun through play, it's important to acknowledge that play is still not available to all. Growing up white and solidly middle class, I had regular meals, a parent available to attend parent-teacher conferences, special trips to such events as a live performance of *Annie*, and access to activities where I could hone the art of play. These affordances were available to me because we were not poor and living in constant fear of whether my parents would lose their jobs if they took time off from work to attend my school events and extracurricular activities.

As a teacher, I remember being sad and upset when one child did beautiful work on our keeping quilt, yet his parents did not attend back-to-school night, where I planned to shower them with praise about their child's work. Later that semester, I was again frustrated when this child's caregivers did not attend parent-teacher conferences or return my phone calls about his excellent insights in class and his passion and great talent for writing. Only later did I learn that his very loving parents worked multiple jobs and were not available at the times I had presented as opportunities to meet. It was not lack of want but lack of access that prevented them from meeting.

When we set up a meeting for six o'clock one morning, I met a beaming father, warily returning from a night shift, whose exhaustion dissolved into pure delight as he learned about his child's great work. These parents were not disengaged, as the common narrative may have you believe, but rather disempowered as a result of working longer hours for less pay just to keep the lights on.

The assumptions we sometimes make as educators about why some parents don't join in the regularly scheduled activities are similar to the assumptions we make about play. We see play as an afterthought, something to do once the real work is done. In my experience, affluent or solidly middle-class white children have plenty of exposure to playful learning, from maker spaces down to well-constructed outdoor play spaces. This isn't true for many of their peers, however.

While there are funds available for low-resourced, largely Black and non-Black communities of color to gain access to tech tools for playful learning or for more experiential learning, the inequitable way in which our schools are funded renders these as extras and not the foundational components they truly are. Additionally, these are the expenses/experiences cut first in low-resourced communities that typically serve Black and non-Black children of color.

Perhaps the narrative of failing schools is really a narrative around access to resources that deeply engage our children in joyful learning. Perhaps our systems are not set up for all children to succeed in the same way.

Let's keep the idea of equity in education at the forefront as we discuss play in the chapters that follow. Let's consider how the lens of equity can be used to ensure every child has access to the resources they need to not only survive, but thrive. Better yet, let's consider how we can use the powerful research presented in the following pages in support of play to advocate for more than equity for our children. Let's use the research, our experiences with our own learners, and the insights of those who have different experiences to advocate for what we all need: justice.

THE INNATELY POWERFUL DESIRE TO PLAY!

Playful learning flips traditional models of instruction to invite into the classroom the creativity and excitement that breed an authentic desire to engage in learning. But what are the roles of teachers and students in this new classroom? And how can we support students in becoming more efficacious and empowered curators of knowledge through play?

In this book, I examine the neurological underpinnings that make the science of learning concrete and unpack the connections between decades of cognitive-science research and playful learning. I'll provide powerful tools for implementing more playful classroom learning to engage students in meaningful acquisition of knowledge about the world around us while transforming passive consumers into active creators of new knowledge.

Each chapter uses cognitive science as an avenue for understanding the mental processes essential for sustained attention and the flexible application of knowledge to solve the complex problems of today and the future. You'll gain clarity around learning theories and discover how to articulate the deep learning that accompanies game play. Vignettes will demonstrate how intentional play in classrooms and living rooms worldwide is anything *but* child's play. Additionally, the chapters are populated with "Level Up" boxes, which provide concrete ways to apply more playful learning to each day to power up your teaching.

The problems of today's world are more complex than ever before, but thankfully the dynamic and engaging nature of play captures some of the essential skills our youngest citizens will need to thrive. The strength of games is their ability to connect us to each other, leveling the playing field and creating space for a shared language in order to work together on whatever comes our way.

When you understand the cognitive science beneath playful learning, you will be able to confidently apply better practices for teaching and learning. Together we'll bring the language of researchers out of journals and into classrooms to support more purposeful and powerful learning each day. The goal of this book is to share lived experiences, high-quality research, and multiple approaches for using games for learning in any learning environment— starting today. Each learner comes to the classroom with their cognitive architecture just begging to be engaged by more playful learning. This book gives you the tools you need to make that happen. Are you ready to get into the game?

MAKING THE GAME

In Romania, children huddle in a circle counting out a rhyme until the *leapşa* is chosen, at which point everyone quickly scatters to avoid being tagged. At the same time in northeastern India, a child is chosen as *magar* (crocodile) and must wade out of the water to tag players on the *denga* (higher ground) who are trying to avoid getting eaten. Whether we call this game *jeu du loup* (wolf game in French), *Shan-Dian-Didi* (lightning in Chinese), or tag (English), most of us have seen, if not played, a similar game.[2]

This is the international language of play. Across the globe, across grades, and across content areas, play knows no borders. In fact, we come to this world with the cognitive architecture in place to learn by doing. Essentially, we are born primed to play! What we've learned about the nature of play is that it helps us see ourselves within larger groups and provides practice negotiating a host of complex roles we'll take on in our lives.[3]

Play is so much more than a vestige of childhood. It's how we've evolved our understanding of the world around us, tested theories of knowledge, and prepared to take on new roles in our changing world. The freedom to play has given us inspiration to actualize some of our greatest dreams, helped us make sense of some of our worst tragedies, and given us an opportunity to find joy in otherwise heartbreaking times.[4]

While I don't entirely agree with A. S. Neill's argument that a child "without adult suggestions of any kind . . . will develop as far as he is capable of developing," I do agree that "children, like adults, learn what they want to learn."[5] As educators we have the unique ability to harness the curiosity, excitement, and eagerness of our learners through play to invite more impactful learning into the classroom.

What's in a Game?

The word *game* has a fascinating etymology. In the 1200s, the Old English *game* meant joy, fun, and amusement. The term's Germanic roots add *glee, merriment*, and *giving a sense of people together* to the definition. Aren't these the very feelings we wish to conjure in our learners and in our own lives?

What's more, the word *game* can be used as a noun (e.g., Good game!), an adjective (e.g., They were game for any challenge!), or a verb (e.g., Game the system). Just as there are many ways to use the word, there are endless opportunities to use games to cultivate unique and more playful learning in your classroom each day!

Before we dig in to the magic of engaging in and co-creating more playful learning experiences, I think it's important to share the way I define some of the constructs and parameters of learning shared in this book. It's useful to consider the strength of language and our own definitions when using terms, including *playful, experiential*, or even *game-based learning*. Each carries tremendous potential to more deeply engage our students in exciting learning.

Playful learning is loosely defined as open-ended and creative experiences of whimsy that incorporate the domains of physical, cognitive, and social-emotional development. Built from the work of Montessori, playful learning does include overall structure and involves objects (or manipulatives) and even lessons. But it also includes student choice and voice, along with collaboration with peers. Moreover, playful learning is driven by intrinsic motivation, and yes, it is defined as FUN!

In contrast with playful learning, *experiential learning* centers on the role of learner as a participant in the process.[6] While experiential learning often builds on the domains of development (physical, cognitive, and social-emotional), it is more guided by intentional practice and seen as a means to an end. Embedded within experiential learning practices is a hallmark reflective piece in which learners consider how the experience connects them to their learning and how their learning connects to the wider world. Experiential learning often includes immersion in real-world experiences, such as visiting town hall and participating during public comment around school policies. Students experience and engage in civic engagement and then reflect, in class, on their role as citizens.

Last is *game-based learning*, which is often confused with gamified learning. Simply put, gamification is replicating the behavior modifications of days gone by under the guise of a game.[7] Instead of popsicle sticks with each child's name that one moves from green to yellow to red, we now have leaderboards, points, and even visible standings within a group. These approaches stem from a system built on compliance, and gamification itself is the use of extrinsic rewards to facilitate engagement.

In contrast, game-based learning recognizes that learning happens through expansive and ever-evolving play. When playing Uno, you reinforce knowledge of colors, numbers, and patterns as you try to be first to get rid of your cards. This often leads to more intrinsically motivated learners who are vested in the activity of collaboration and play and not focused on the external rewards (although winning against my oldest son is still quite a feat!).

The single most important distinction between game-based learning and gamification is that game-based learning is playful. Most game-based learning experiences are also low stakes, iterative, and imaginative. What's more, games are potentially community-building and joyful learning experiences. Gamification in the form of popcorn math or round-robin reading where students get points triggers anxiety in some, competition in others, and mostly nervous groans. So, let's ditch the forced and anxiety-inducing models of gamification, whether it's the stoplight behavior chart or digitized worksheets being passed off as games, and instead seek out ways to create authentic, engaging, and co-created, playful experiences that drive deeper learning.

A good game draws us in for many reasons. Games can be challenging, fun (even funny!), competitive, and complex. Players often have multiple pathways toward achieving a game's goal, and there are games to meet all types of needs and interests. For example, both card games like Uno, in which players practice rudimentary numeracy and literacy skills, and virtual reality–based simulations like *Beat Saber*, in which participants hone spatial, rhythmic, and sensory skills, allow students to explore content while learning to relate to others. Perhaps you've been taught to consider these kinds of games as something students get to do after they've finished sit-and-get learning, but decades of research show that play is, in fact, the most powerful kind of learning the very content you are trying to teach!

PINBALL WIZARDS AND THE NEURAL CIRCUITRY OF US

Humans are hardwired to learn. In fact, it takes an awful lot for us *not* to constantly acquire new information. Even when just passively sitting and observing the world around you, you're learning about the people, places, and activities in your field of vision. Will you do anything with that knowledge? Well, that's up to you! But how *do* we actually learn?

The brain is the origin of our every thought, move, and feeling. It not only regulates our breathing without our active participation but also sets the stage for any actions we consciously and subconsciously take. The specialized cells that make up our central nervous system are called *neurons*. Neuroscientists estimate that at birth a newborn has roughly one hundred billion neurons, which are strengthened and pruned throughout life largely based on how and when they are used.[8]

New tools allow researchers to study groups of neurons that become neural networks and together form the basis of our current behavior and may even predict our future health.[9] Tools have evolved from the original Golgi staining, which allowed scientists to observe neurons under a microscope, to newer methods that allow scientists to stain entire dendritic trees, the roots branching from the soma, or cell body. By studying the neurons in our brain, scientists have found that complex networks of neurons continue to form throughout life. These nerve cells in your brain, or cerebral cortex, that carry human thought also grow and change throughout our lives. This is the foundation for the idea of neural plasticity.

The way in which the brain grows and reorganizes as we grow helps us become more efficient learners. Each of our neurons is surrounded by many tiny arms called *dendrites*. Each dendrite is sensitive to certain chemicals in its environment, and when enough of those chemicals are sensed by dendrites, they send an electrical signal through the cell, which is transmitted across the longer arms, called *axons*. Chemical signals from the axon of one cell are received by the dendrites of a neighboring cell through *synapses*. These chemical reactions, in which synapses send messages between neurons, are the physical manifestation of learning. Our body also has an incredible way of insulating those synapses in a process called *myelination*. Conversely, connections that are not used are pruned, just like the wilting leaves of a plant can be clipped to make the plant grow stronger.

Neural connections across cerebral cortices are continuously reinforced and strengthened when they are activated in synchrony.[10] This means that each time you practice a skill, whether it be playing chess or calculating math formulas, you are strengthening the connections between neurons, creating rich networks across neurons that control different regions of your mind and body. Both playing chess and solving math problems activate neurons in the prefrontal cortex—where thought originates—along with neurons that direct hand movement, telling your hand to move the pawn or transcribe a calculation of Pythagorean's theorem.

While connections between neural networks are strengthened when used, over time, the brain also gets rid of unnecessary connections to make way for ongoing learning and efficiency of processing. These exciting neurological developments begin the moment we join the world, and they are activated through interaction—largely through experiential play!

This process of myelination and pruning not only helps us become more efficient learners but also provides ample evidence for the "use it or lose it" rule of applying learning to secure learning. The idea of deliberate practice, or even "grit," is the application of neuroscience. Learning takes place when a learner has access to meaningful information and the opportunity to practice. When neurons are activated together, they form rich neural networks. When neurons are not activated, they are not helpful for future learning and are pruned. Exciting new neurological research is beginning to show evidence that cultivating our students' level of task persistence may actually impact neuroanatomy![11]

As a child of the '80s, I spent much of my time at the arcade, which was the place to be. In metro Detroit, where I grew up, we'd head straight for the Eight Ball Deluxe at Tally Hall. It wasn't a whiz-bang pinball machine with fancy artwork and wild and crazy sounds. Rather, it was an old standby that was challenging and beautiful enough to keep me and my friends engaged while also accessible enough to help us feel like we got better with each try. After stacking our quarters along one side of the machine, we'd stand back and wait for our turn.

Watching the ball launch from the plunger and into the playing field required the greatest patience, and when it was my turn, I felt my reflexes engage as I watched the ball come into play. Mrs. Abbott's trigonometry lessons came to life as I estimated where the ball would hit the flippers after bouncing off the bumpers. Each time I hit a target, the connections between neurons across visual, auditory, and motor regions were strengthened. In turn, these neural networks strengthened connections between the physics of potential energy, circuits, and momentum within my neocortex. The skills of patience and perseverance can be found in playing pinball, along with the skills of physics and trigonometry.

Pinball required both skill and a bit of luck to refine and hone my ability over time. With each new high score, I felt proud of my accomplishment, but also eager to try to do better the next time. Caught up in playing, little did I know the complex neural networking happening in my adolescent brain. Those multiple microcalculations I was performing to determine how to tap the flippers to keep the ball out of the drain were reinforcing the connections, or synapses, between neurons and enhancing my newly connected neural networks.

It would be decades before the idea of grit would come to the fore in our culture, and decades still to find evidence the that pruning of unused synapses between neurons encourages use of successful skills over less-successful ones. Much like a pinball machine, our neural networks both help secure knowledge acquisition and make us more curious learners!

HARDWIRED TO LEARN

Learning scientists have studied how people learn by looking at the three main domains, or areas, of human development: *cognitive, social-emotional*, and *physical*. As we grow, these three areas grow at different paces and work to support one another. For instance, as an infant reaches for and learns to grasp a rattle (physical), she develops a mental framework, or *schema*, for how to reach out for the rattle while connecting the exploration to the curious and enjoyable sound it makes in her hands (cognitive). When the child drops the rattle and launches into tears, it is the response of the caregiver that sets the stage for secure attachment, knowing she will be cared for when she cries out (social-emotional), now and in her future.

During game play, students apply what they know (cognitive) to work (physical) toward a shared (social-emotional) end goal. When I was playing pinball at Tally Hall, I had to calculate where the ball might hit the flippers as it bounced off kickers and targets to plan (cognitive) for the ideal moment to hit those flippers and launch it back into play (physical), all while placing those quarters along the side of the machine to play again despite my disappointment (social-emotional) if for some reason I didn't earn that end-of-ball bonus.

As educators, we have countless spaces and places, both within the curriculum and within the broader area of child development, to challenge our students to grow across social-emotional, cognitive, and physical domains. Level Up 1 provides just a few of the many examples of how games can engage and enhance learning throughout the curriculum and across age groups. Of course, we also learn through music and art, dance, and movement, and even when we're quietly reflecting, such as in a game of chess.

| LEVEL UP 1 ||||
| ENGAGING THE DOMAINS OF HUMAN DEVELOPMENT WITH GAMES IN THE CLASSROOM ||||
Age Group	Social-Emotional	Cognitive	Physical
Early Childhood (birth to K)	Science: Taking turns while playing a game of Sneaky, Snacky Squirrel	English Language Arts (ELA): Identifying letters and words to win the game of Zingo!	Recess: Refining fine and gross motor skills while playing cornhole
Childhood (K–5)	ELA: Taking the perspective of others while playing Apples to Apples	Math: Calculating probabilities of the beans that will win you the most points in Bohnanza	Gym: Developing hand-eye coordination in wall ball
Middle School (6–8)	Math: Learning flexibility and advance planning through Monopoly	History: Learning combat strategies of world leaders through the lens of chess	Science: Competing in teams to geo-tag indigenous species of plants around the school with iNaturalist
High School (9–12)	History: Improving negotiation skills through Settlers of Catan	Math: Honing analytic problem solving and attention to details through Mancala	History: Hide riddles about the history of your town, school, neighborhood, with WallaMe and be the first to solve the puzzle.

SUPERBOSS-LEVEL ASSESSMENTS: WATCH THEM PLAY!

Teachers are constantly observing the students, and often the most interesting observations occur outside the classroom. As a primary school teacher, I would pick up my kids on the blacktop each morning and walk them to class, which gave me a chance to observe them interacting with their peers or caregivers. Taking my kids to lunch or picking them up from recess gave me additional time to observe how they engaged with others and how they maneuvered their social-emotional needs through their cognitive skills within a physical space. When the specials teachers came to my room, I wouldn't always leave to prep for the next period but would often engage in busywork that would allow me to watch the dynamics of different students as they engaged with one another as another grown-up entered the room. Observing students in class or during lunch or recess can inform our interactions with our kids, and if we're lucky, we'll help them see how learning lives everywhere and doesn't always look like a textbook!

Secondary teachers have the opportunity to observe students between classes as they talk with peers in the hallway, demonstrating their ability to regulate their emotions (social-emotional). Maybe they'll share insights from a recently viewed episode of *The Walking Dead*, hypothesizing how they would prepare to prevent a zombie apocalypse (cognitive). For a teacher on the lookout, these observations could inspire a unit on emergency preparedness through examining the history of pandemics, complete with the potential for a role-playing game, or perhaps a lesson on neurological development in a biology class where students learn about the role of the cerebellum in motor function and how it might affect zombies' movement.

Game play invites creativity and reflection and doesn't require the teacher to be a sage on the stage but rather a fluid guide-on-the-side. As in a battle with a "superboss," a term for the more difficult-to-defeat enemies in video games, you may not win every time, but you always learn. In fact, standing back to observe how your kids attempt novel ways to overthrow superbosses is itself an exercise in patience and gradual release. And if you can level up to this point, what you see will amaze and inspire you. You'll be able to observe and document dynamic learning and progress of students outside of tests and standardized assessments. Why should observations be relegated to early childhood classrooms when all our learners are demonstrating powerful learning outside of a single test score? This should be celebrated with the student, shared with caregivers, and used to shift the paradigm from formative assessments of rote content to those that include the development of the whole child.

Level Up 2 provides a flexible template for recalling, sharing, and celebrating the achievements of students across domains and content areas. This is a valuable tool for discussing a student's growth with parents, especially during back-to-school nights or conferences. Using Google sheets, you can create a single document, with space for each student, where you can jot down small notes as you move throughout the classroom, making observations. Ideally you will find a few minutes after dismissal each day to quickly enter these comments. It shouldn't take more than five minutes and will help show you which students you've been able to observe and identify those who may need additional attention. You'll find yourself congratulating students for their accomplishments, boosting their sense of efficacy, and encouraging them to engage even more in learning each day. What's more? Come parent-teacher conference you'll be able to report on positive attributes across physical and social-emotional learning, rather than just progress on cognitive skills.

LEVEL UP 2 SEEING THE WHOLE STUDENT			
Student	Social-Emotional	Cognitive	Physical
Emily T. Fourth Grade *(e.g., student name and grade here)*	9/21/19: During music class, students were playing red light/ green light when Emily noticed Ryan's shoe was untied and stopped the game to help. *(e.g., date, location, observation)*	11/2/2019: During math, students were playing Swish when Emily noticed she could make a four-way swish by overlapping multiple cards, demonstrating advanced spatial awareness. *(e.g., date, location, observation)*	1/27/2020: Playing Jenga during indoor recess, Emily showed improved fine-motor skills in maneuvering the blocks, exceeding her Individual Education Program (IEP) goals for physical therapy (PT). *(e.g., date, location, observation)*

With games, however, it is not just the teacher assessing the students. The power of games is that they let learners lead! They also allow students to celebrate one another using their own voice. In Level Up 3, student voice and experience are honored through game play. Asking students across primary or secondary classrooms to identify an MVP during game play, or in any part of the day, places students behind the wheel. When one student requests an "instant replay" because their peer has done something awesome, everyone wins, and the culture of the class shifts. The unique characteristics of your classroom will change the way you approach Level Up 3, but the goal is to get all students to be self- and peer-celebrating by seeing, calling out, and applauding the best in one another. This opportunity should be afforded to all our learners. As self-directed agents of their own learning, this builds a sense of efficacy and empowers students. Using their own voices, our students see that they are valued members of our classroom and citizens of the world who are already whole and able to provide meaningful feedback to improve their lived experiences.

LEVEL UP 3 STUDENT VOICE I'D LIKE TO REQUEST AN INSTANT REPLAY...	
MVP	**The awesomeness I witnessed was when. . .**
Emily T. *(e.g., student name here)*	Emily and I were playing Catan when she out-strategized me by using a completely new strategy of going for a port instead of going for the largest army!

CREATING THROUGH ITERATION, LEARNING THROUGH DOING

Play is by nature lower stakes than traditional learning, and the originative nature of play and games invites the stick-with-it-ness that builds confidence and competence. King Bowser of Koopa Troopa fame beat you again? No worries—look out for his tricks next time and replay that round. But that's not just the case for a game of *Super Mario*; the same lesson holds for a player folding proteins in Foldit, a citizen-science game in which players around the world complete puzzles to earn the highest number of points. Beyond points, the successful completion of these puzzles also brings bench scientists closer to understanding the very nature of proteins and, ultimately, the eradication of diseases. Through this game, players are not only learning complex content like molecular biology, design, and sustainability, but they are also constantly working to solve more complex problems than they did previously. There are no failures, only setbacks that will fill their cognitive toolbox with new strategies for solving problems in the future. Those buzzwords *grit*, *mindset*, and *perseverance*? Yep. They're in there too. The originative nature of truly engaging play parallels the way scientists seek out cures for painful diseases and the way engineers design solutions for our centuries-old architecture.

Games can be played solo or with hundreds of people, from friends and neighbors nearby to people across the globe. Listen in as a middle schooler strategically plans an attack on Tilted Towers in *Fortnite*. You'll hear how individual players organize their cross-continental squad and emerge with a Victory Royale, winning as the last remaining player, duo, squad, or team. Watch as an elementary-age child *mods* (modifies) the skin, clothes, and accessories their player avatar wears in *Minecraft* to create their own vision of what school could be in an open-source game with other children from across the nation and around the world.

The limitless possibilities for connecting, growing, and joyful expression through play are palpable, as are the opportunities to learn from others and take important learning risks.

So how can we leverage the intrigue and excitement of play to level up learning? Perhaps the first step is to look at the games you loved to play as a child, as well as the games you love to play now. Even more important is taking the time to find out what games your students are already playing.

Level Up 4 guides you to discover what kinds of play your students enjoy. As you ask students questions about the games they play, think about similarities and differences in student answers. Don't forget to consider the distinctions between the games you mention and those your students mention. What are the similarities among games you list and the ones your students list? What new games have you never heard of before?

LEVEL UP 4
WHO'S GOT GAME?

- What kinds of games do you play?
- What is it about each of the games that you love?
- How do each of these games make you feel?
- Who are the people you like to play games with?
- When do you typically play games?
- What games do you really not like playing?
- What is it about those games that you don't like?
- What games do you wish you knew more about?
- What would you like to know? Why?
- If you could bring any game into class to play for a day, what would it be, how would you share it, and what would you hope your classmates would see about that game?

As you review the games your students name in Level Up 4, think about how you might bring these games into your classroom. Think about how your learners can use the games to amplify their voices as unique individuals and share their superpowers with the class. Consider how you might invite students to use the games they recommend to lead new learning experiences by demonstrating their skill and inviting in others. What it is about the experiences students share that they love most? It may not be simply about defeating the Ender Dragon in *Minecraft*; it may also be about how the game helps them connect or feel a sense of efficacy. Think about ways you can together modify existing games to build community. Be open to the possibility of discovering novel ways to connect content to game play, creating novel learning experiences. In each consideration, you are actively honoring the diverse voices and interests of learners in your classroom. With an eye toward inclusion and diversity, where everyone is invited to play and all voices are heard, you can provide access to more authentic and enjoyable learning for all your learners. What's more, you are allowing students to see learning as a continued journey of growth, innovation, reflection, and persistence. In this way, you are propelling your students further into a future fueled by a sense of efficacy and an ability to connect meaningfully with those around them.

An expert in the field of learning games, Dr. Karen Schrier has published extensively on the various ways to map existing games into differ-ent contexts to enhance learning. In *Learning, Education & Games, Volume 3: 100 Games to Use in the Classroom & Beyond*, Schrier pro-vides summaries, logistical considerations, and curricular connections for more than one hun-dred games. What's more, each game provides connections to support the development of the uniquely human skills of perspective taking and creativity.

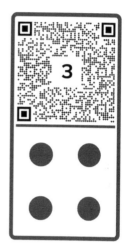

You can instantly increase your experience points (XP in gamer speak) in this free resource accessible online via ETC Press (scan QR code for quick access!). Explore games that may be new to you, such as *A Normal Lost Phone*, or widely known games your students have likely enjoyed for years, such as *Minecraft*. With help from this vital text you can, for example, connect a one-hour adventure seeking the owner of a lost phone to lessons on ethical decision making and identity in an ELA classroom or within a unit on social justice.

The purpose of this book is not to repeat the decades of rich literature available from Schrier and others but instead to provide connections between the science of learning and the applied practice of teaching through the lens of games and playful, experiential learning.[12,13,14,15] For far too long, the cognitive science has lived in an isolated ivory tower, never meeting the needs of the more than one billion school-aged chil-dren around the globe.

Using What We Know to Help Us Grow

Neuroscience shows that we are truly hardwired to learn. Our desire to connect, collaborate, and create enhances our humanity. The games we play encourage these connections and collaborations and, if done well, even our creations. By understanding how playing games maps on to how we live, love, and work, we can use games as a template to support students who will be more confident learners tomorrow than they were yesterday.

Game play is far more than growing stronger brains; it's about building healthier lives and embracing the whole child and the whole community. Research shows that outdoor play and physical activity strongly impact cognitive and physical development. In a study conducted in Italy, more than four hundred children aged five to ten years were engaged in a six-month randomized intervention based around play.[16] While guided play through a more traditional physical education class increased specific hand-eye motor skills, it was the free outdoor play that truly amplified the children's cognitive, physical, and perhaps even social-emotional development. Additional research has shown that playful learning experiences—from yoga to Pilates to physical activity on the playground—enhances the executive functioning of children aged four to twelve years.[17,18]

The impact of movement on the healthy growth of our neural networks cannot be understated. This means that including more physical play may be the answer we seek to support our learners in honing their uniquely human traits. Taken together, the data from these studies show that learning through play is a powerful way to help the brain maximize its natural plasticity to grow and acquire knowledge through sensory-motor input.[19]

As policy makers fret over the future of work and learning, the constant struggle is to identify exactly *how* we humans fit into the picture. What will our role be when ever-evolving technology takes on the rote work and, perhaps later, the more creative work we think of as our uniquely human domain? The answer may be a strong foundation of flexible skills rooted in play that will help us maneuver complex scenarios.

YOUR ROLE IN THE GAME

So what now? Perhaps you'll be inspired to invite your students to bring their favorite games into the classroom and find ways that game play maps on to the learning you're doing together this year. Can students explain why the map in *Fortnite* changes each season, using evidence from a science lesson? Are students able to explain the trajectory of *Angry Birds* as a result of learning done in math or physics? Can learners understand the multiple perspectives of characters in What Remains of Edith Finch, thus demonstrating their understanding of social-emotional skills, decision making, and context from a high school English class?

The answer to each of these questions is a resounding YES! And the best news is that if done properly, learning through play will bring students to these conclusions themselves, with you as their guide-on-the-side, while they develop a deeper sense of autonomy and efficacy in themselves as learners.

Then, once empowered, your students may be ready to move from playing games as they are to creating their own games, demonstrating how much they have learned. Maybe your students will modify the beloved game of Uno to better recall equivalent fractions in math. Or perhaps your learners are ready to recreate Scrabble with elements from the periodic table as component pieces. Students could even create their own version of Pokémon to demonstrate the evolution of characters in a text and how they use their superpowers to overcome obstacles. With your support, learners can see that in creating their own learning experiences, they are able to connect with others, solve real problems, and maybe even change the world.

RULES OF ENGAGEMENT

I t was a crisp October afternoon and likely one of the last sunny and warm days of the fall. I decided to cut short my planning period during the students' lunchtime and head down to the blacktop to observe my kids during recess. There I saw three groups of students standing off to the side of the play space, deeply engaged in some sort of debate.

Suddenly a child in the middle of the far group broke away from the crowd. It was Leslie, a confident learner in our classroom known for her strong voice and kind ear toward her peers. All three groups grew silent and watched as she proceeded to run to the far end of the play space, tag the wall, run to the opposite end of the play space to tag that wall, and ultimately head back to her original group. When she returned, they converged to make a single larger group.

Debate and discussion followed when two other children, Kimberly and Louis, appeared to propose a different iteration to the game. Kimberly ran to the far wall while Louis ran to the perpendicular wall. Kimberly ran from the far wall to the wall where Louis stood with his hand held out at the ready. Once tagged, Louis ran to the far wall and looked back at Kimberly, who gave him an approving nod.

Together the two ran back to the group, and the children burst into an even more heated discussion just as the monitor blew her whistle: recess was over. Running to our class spot on the blacktop, my kids formed a line and happily greeted me: "Hi, Ms. Blau!" Rosy cheeked and bright eyed, my students exuded joy after playing in the fresh air.

Intrigued by what I'd seen, I said, "That looked like a fun game you were playing. What's it called?"

"Oh, we weren't playing the game yet," Kimberly responded. "We were just figuring out the rules."

I was taken aback by her statement. Surely, they were playing a game. There was turn-taking, purposeful and active movement, and a group of kids eagerly watching to see what the others would do next. It was then that I recalled the research of Vygotsky, discussed only a week prior during my own graduate class.

Divergent Thinking in Action

Pioneering developmental psychologist Lev Vygotsky (1896–1934) is renowned for his work showing that social interaction is fundamental to cognitive development. That our interactions with those around us— including peers, parents, and teachers—shapes the way we understand the world around us and its limits and possibilities. When my grad school colleagues and I first met Vygotsky, we spent a lively hour discussing the proposition of rules and play as essential elements of child development. Through play, young learners come to understand cultural norms, and through establishing the rules of play, they establish their relationships with one another. In our discussion, we also unpacked the idea that the way we determine our roles in a shared space guides our agreements for how we'll work toward achieving a common goal.

What I had witnessed on the playground was Vygotsky in action.[20] My kids had, without direction, collaborated to decide on the parameters of their play and, in doing so, had gained a shared language and shared direction for moving forward. Setting up boundaries and rules and then testing those rules is one of the things that makes games so powerful.

What I found most fascinating in watching my kiddos spend the entire recess creating rules is the juxtaposition of being freed and also being constrained by the boundaries (rules) of the game. My students literally spent the entire recess planning for play that never happened. Instead they focused on the process of mutual agreement that was foundational to their play and is, frankly, essential to our work together as humans. At seven years old, in second grade, they had already tapped into knowledge that many people much older than them still struggle with. If educators took the time to watch kids at play, they'd find that we don't need to whale students with standards requiring they learn how to demonstrate the four Cs; critical thinking, communication, collaboration, and creativity are already embedded in the authentic and shared experience of play.

What if we're trying too hard to fit young humans into a series of triangles as they acquire the "foundational" knowledge we believe is essential for development when they're already shaped like the stars we hope they'll one day become? If we shift our perspective, is it possible we'll see that kids are showing *us* how to learn best: how to collaborate with others, how to navigate tricky situations, how to keep going even if it hurts? I always think about watching my own children learn to walk. How many times did they fall before they walked?

Guided and free play are powerful ways of engaging students in learning and also give our kids a break from what has become a mechanized system of education. But it is not just the play itself that is both freeing and rich with critical learning opportunities. Setting up the boundaries of the game through the rules we create invites a critical process of both divergent and convergent thinking that is uniquely human. The process of calibrating each learner's individual goals with those of others—seeing where they come together and where they are distinct—sets the foundation for social skills requisite for meaningful debate and perspective taking.

Establishing rules requires both convergent and divergent thinking. When learners are engaged in divergent thinking, they see different ways of approaching ideas and solutions as well as how to connect with others who think differently. Often connected to creativity, divergent thinking is associated with the various perspectives students bring to the table when navigating play.[21] And while divergent thinking or multiple perspectives helps create ideas that will become the rules or boundaries for game play, convergent thinking is required to come to shared agreements.

Shared agreements are born from acknowledgment of divergent thoughts as well as those that are aligned, or convergent. What do we care about most? How can we hold one another accountable for keeping these agreements? When agreeing on the rules of play, our learners are navigating complex relational skills. They are also enacting high-level executive functioning skills to develop a shared understanding.

How Context Shapes the Construction of Knowledge

Watching students navigate the rules on the ballcourt or playground, we learn that student conversations center on how the world should and could work. What's more, when our students take part in creating the rules of play, they have a voice in creating the world they'd like to live in. These experiences do not need to be relegated to the playground. They can be brought into the classroom, where allowing students to discuss and help form the rules of engagement can facilitate more authentic and engaged learning. It also invites critical conversations about the content and contexts in which we all live, learn, and grow.

Critical in the development of a sense of self is the exploration of identity. While games lower the stakes for this type of exploration, the larger societal mores are often superimposed before the game even begins. Like the rules of the game, societal norms often determine who gets access to knowledge that impacts who ultimately sits at the table where decisions are made. It's important to talk about the rules of game play as shared agreements, and you can have an interesting conversation with students about who wrote the rules, how just those rules are for all involved, and how we might change those rules if we hope to create a more equitable society. These are intense conversations for certain, but they are essential if we are going to tip the scale toward justice.

The rules we create through play can model our beliefs and amplify our understanding of the world around us. In games, these rules can deepen understanding across contexts and content. When we allow our learners to bring their most beloved learning experiences into the classroom, as suggested in Level Up 4, their interests are validated and valued. In the world of play, there is often less fear of repercussion and more of an opportunity to try something new and exciting. Play also invites student voice and choice, something we'll dig even deeper into in Chapter 3.

The nature of games, from role-playing adventures to scavenger hunts, invites the co-creation of rules and multiple ways for students to move and think while playing. For example, role-playing games like No Thank You, Evil! require students to develop characters and backstories that will ultimately impact the rules for game play. In an open-creation game such as *Minecraft*, the shared rules determine the nature and method of inquiry, whether players are exploring ancient lands or creating a structure capable of transporting two thousand villagers across the Pacific Ocean. Then there are scavenger hunt games for which digital tools like WallaMe allow you to hide messages on walls in the classroom, the school building, or even throughout the town. Following clues revealed on each wall by the WallaMe app, students collaborate while moving from location to location, working together to solve a complex and exciting puzzle.

Regardless of the modality—imagination, paper, or even newfangled technology—games offer important opportunities to discuss the parameters or rules for engagement. Level Up 5 presents questions that offer insight into how different modes of learning may be a more authentic approach to teaching traditional content. Moreover, the questions in Level Up 5 should prompt you to discover experiences never before available to our students, from immersive time travel through history to journeys across the universe. For example, wouldn't a scavenger hunt with secret messages left across the school building be a fun way for rising sixth graders to learn about their new school while also making new friends and preparing for an entirely new school experience?

LEVEL UP 5
MULTIPLE MODES TO AUTHENTIC LEARNING

- Can a role-playing game increase perspective taking?
- Can an open-creation game improve spatial awareness skills?
- Can a scavenger hunt help students learn a new space?
- Can a virtual tour provide access to a far-off place?
- Can a guessing game invite conversation about systems and histories?

DESIGNING AND DEFINING OUR SHARED SPACE

If you ever ask Google, *Why do all coffee shops look alike?* the search engine will return billions of results.[22] Much of what you will find are laments and declarations that the "hipster aesthetic is taking over" coffee shops everywhere. If you dive deeper, however, you'll find something much more interesting than what you see at first glance.

If you're a coffee drinker, it's likely that your goal when you enter a coffee shop is to move as quickly as possible to consuming your coffee. You don't want to waste time figuring out how to order or where to find the cream and sugar. Luckily for you, that goal is shared by most of your fellow coffee drinkers, leading to shared, if unspoken, agreements about how to best expedite and perhaps improve our coffee drinking experience. Thus, whether you're at your favorite coffee shop or in a new-to-you coffee shop anywhere from Tucson to Tuscaloosa, your previous experience with coffee shops helps you find the accoutrements needed to jazz up your java.

The reason you know where to find cream and sugar for your coffee in an entirely new space a testament to cognitive science. The idea that each of us has mental models for scenarios we've experienced over time is at the heart of psychologist Jean Piaget's theory of cognitive development.[23] These models are called *schema* and can be thought of as flexible blueprints that are based on our own experiences in the world. This is why when you got behind the steering wheel of a car for the very first time you understood how it worked because you had likely spent many years as a passenger. Your mental models, or schemas, are based on experiences and serve as guideposts in navigating both similar and new experiences.

Shared rules for shared experiences help us navigate in known and unknown situations and help us organize our knowledge as we learn and grow. When we acquire new information that easily fits within our mental models it's called *assimilation*. For instance, my son exhibited assimilation when he pointed to a tiger in a book and called it a cat. However, when we're presented with new information that challenges our mental models it's called *accommodation*, as our mental models must shift to incorporate a new understanding. So while a tiger is in the feline family, it was important for me to explain that the tiger was actually not the same as our tabby cat and was far more dangerous.

Our mental models, or schemas, for finding the condiment station in a coffee shop or distinguishing between friendly domesticated creatures and potentially deadly big cats are no different from the models we use to navigate games.

While my students worked to define the rules or parameters of their game play during recess, their unique experiences and histories played a role in how they wanted to see the game play out. In learning experiences, we share agreements for working and learning in a shared space. Innovative educators are no longer using traditional rules but instead seeking student input to find the supports that will help students learn more effectively and navigate learning the way we navigate the coffee shop.

In Level Up 6, the parameters for game play help us see how our students grapple with new information simply by the way they navigate the rules. What's more, the process of setting parameters shows how students perceive the world around them and even what drives their learning. In asking, "What's the goal?" we're checking for understanding and learning about what matters most to each player. In Monopoly, your goal is simply to not go bankrupt. The last player standing wins. But to what end?

LEVEL UP 6
WHAT'S THE GOAL

- What's the goal of the game?
- How do we want to get to that goal?
- What can we use to play the game?
- How flexible are we in the way we get to our goal?
- Who and where can we seek support if we're stuck?
- When do we know it's over?
- When and where can we invite play into every day?

The way our students establish rules helps identify new games to play and how shared agreements are made in the classroom. On the playground, Kimberly and Louis extended Leslie's suggested rules for the game. A simple game of tag turned into a relay race. As Leslie, Kimberly, and Louis discussed the rules to their game of chase, the goal was clear: to be the first group to finish the race. However, the path they'd take to doing that was not yet defined. This leads to question two as outlined in

Level Up 6: How do we want to get there? Some of the kids wanted to touch just the far wall and run back. Others said they loved the idea of changing the game so they could do a relay with more friends.

Watching our students come up with the rules to their games is an exciting way to understand what matters most to our learners. It also allows educators to participate in the design of the rules of our collective engagement and models the navigation of complex problem solving. This ability is foundational for learning how to work together, even to build consensus. Moreover, in defining the rules for engagement, students can learn to take the field of vision (FOV), or perspective, of others. As well as being an essential skill in creating clear and compelling visual games, this also develops the ability to see outside oneself and potentially develop empathy for others.

In my book *Designed to Learn: Using Design Thinking to Bring Purpose and Passion to the Classroom*, I dive into the discussion on why educators can never get to Bloom's taxonomy of learning before addressing Maslow's hierarchy of needs. In short, relationships and shared goals must be established before deep learning experiences can occur. Teachers must be trusted adults in the lives of our students before we can work together to create playful learning experiences that are both deeply engaging and empowering. The road to becoming those trusted adults includes involving our students in the creation of shared rules for our shared space. This process of developing shared rules is often embedded in our classroom culture, but it is more authentically apparent in how our children navigate play. Watching kids play, we see that parameters for play are often intuitive, and they are more readily accepted when they are co-created. Following our students' lead in defining the parameters of our shared space has the potential to also enrich our connections to one another in the classroom and provide safety for our kids to take risks in learning.

Collaborating with students in defining and designing rules ensures that you're using your teacher magic to support your students in the best possible way. You are seen as an ally in helping learners as they seek out the supplies and spaces for playful learning. Collaboration as an educator with learners as they co-create playful learning ensures that authentic and meaningful learning can happen in schools each day, especially if you are creating your own games in the classroom.

NOT JUST WHY, WHY NOT?

Asking students to define the goal of their play is more than the question of how you win; it's the question of what matters to each player. What I didn't mention in the above vignette is how Lorenzo pleaded for one team to race one at a time, whereas Bobbie Jo wanted every team to begin simultaneously at the sound of the whistle.

On the surface, this seemed a small request. Then Lorenzo shared his reasoning: he wanted his friends to be able to see him race. Think about that: he wanted to be seen. As we listen to our kids navigate the rules of their games, we are invited to witness their innermost hopes and goals. And if we listen closely, we also will discover their innermost motivations. The motivation or drive to play a game is often our why, but sometimes it's the "why not" that shows us what our learners care about most of all.

Behavior is impacted by internal and external pressures, which some might call motivation. *Intrinsic motivation* is that which drives us from within and is the impetus for feeling purposeful, whereas *extrinsic motivation* is something outside ourselves that drives us to act—for example, grades, test scores, degrees.

These tangible outcomes are largely extrinsic yet can still be intrinsically motivating, based on the individual. For instance, some students are driven by the sense of accomplishment a letter grade brings. Others acquire a sense of accomplishment from simply participating.

The reasons students find specific rules for game play important can be driven by either intrinsic or extrinsic motivation. Regardless, what I find most interesting are the conversations that start with *why not*. For instance, why not change the rules so multiple teams run at once? Why does it really matter to both Bobbie Jo and Lorenzo? Moreover, asking these questions allows students to navigate seemingly discrete goals and emerge with a better perspective of each other.

So when creating the rules of engagement, it is important to look not only at the why of the game, learning experience, or project, but also the why not. Why is it important to some students that a specific number of students be at a center in the classroom or on a team? Understanding what matters most provides an authentic way to assess the nature of relationships among students. It is also a way to create a shared language and shared goals that help students communicate their needs and their own understanding of their social relationships.

What struck me as I listened to my students debate over the rules of a game they had not yet played was how social hierarchies shifted and evolved. It was impressive that students were so set on playing this game the next day, despite not knowing what the game might actually look like. Ultimately, my students would spend the rest of the week playing and then updating the rules, resulting in a fascinating set of discussions that demonstrates another interesting aspect of learning science: the power of a model.

As each of my students presented a rationale for what seemed to an outsider to be small changes, they were really aligning goals and perhaps developing a deeper perspective as an "other." My kids were learning to take the perspective of their peers. For instance, how many players would run in a relay seemed to me a minor consideration, yet it became a topic of great debate as my students attempted to create balanced teams. It was fascinating to watch as one child explained the importance of counting the amount of time each child ran their part of the course in order to keep the teams "fair," while another child was adamant about counting the time for the overall team.

Upon closer observation, I noticed how students listened with intent and seemed to look for ways to calibrate their expectations with that of their peers. In a sense, our students are moving beyond developing efficacy as they form shared rules and toward the ability to take the perspective of and perhaps even develop empathy for others.

Navigating complex relationships makes creating shared rules even more complex. A pioneer in the field of self-efficacy, psychologist Albert Bandura described how our perceptions about ourselves and how we see ourselves as compared with others vary across different areas of our work.[24] As an educator, you have likely seen how your students perceive themselves in comparison with others impacts their beliefs about themselves.

This is a powerful psychological construct that can change the way our students learn in the classroom and will follow them into their lives outside the school walls. Each of our beliefs about our own ability, or self-efficacy, has the potential to change not only how we behave in certain situations but also how we approach situations in the future. While we'll explore self-efficacy on the personal level further in Chapter 3 and the impact of peer models on beliefs about one's own ability in Chapter 4, it is important to note that students look to others when calibrating their expectations and defining shared rules.[25]

Understanding the role each student takes during physical play may also map the type of relationships your learners have with one another and inform how they see themselves represented in the classroom. While elementary students have more organized games during recess, secondary students demonstrate preferences in the way they engage in free play. These preferences help us understand their social networks and thus their priorities for engaging with peers. Moreover, this information can be used to support you as their teacher as you facilitate experiences inside the classroom that augment relationships, reinforce skills, and enrich the experiences of each student.

Leveling up in games means gaining experience points, or XP. And games give you a perfect way to demonstrate this IRL (in real life). So if you're ready to earn some serious XP IRL, Level Up 7 can support you in seeking out how students identify with peers and making some interesting connections about which voices are and are not heard.

LEVEL UP 7
CO-CREATION & PERSPECTIVE TAKING

- Who names the game?
- How did each of the rules come into play?
- To whom was each rule important?
- Which peers agreed with the rules?
- Which peers disagreed with the rules?
- Which players do students want on their teams?
- Which players do students not want on their teams?
- What does each student bring to the game?

As you look at the way your students self-organize and the way they organize while under the watchful supervision of a supportive teacher (that's you!), you can begin to map the dynamic relationships of learners in your classroom. For instance, whose voices consistently rise to the top to name the game? How are rules of engagement defined and honed inside and outside the four walls of your classroom and by whom? How do peer groups navigate disagreements during unsupervised learning and activity time, from recess to center time? As you reflect on how rules are made, shared, and revised inside and outside the classroom, you will find ways to support each child in having a voice in the way the rules of playing and learning together are enacted.

Teacher Perceptions and Our Rules of Engagement

The impact of self-efficacy is not only important to our learners but also to us as lifelong learners, as the way we see ourselves in others continues to impact the way we perceive our own ability. As a teacher educator in New York City, I would facilitate a shared experience before jumping into the research by Bandura. The goal was to demonstrate the impact of models on not only our students but also on us as the grown-ups in the room.

To begin this experience, I would ask for a show of hands in response to the following question: How many of you feel very confident in your ability to calculate the sum of two double-digit numbers in your head? I would then ask for two volunteers who felt fairly confident in their ability to complete this seemingly simple task. Then I would ask all the other teachers in the room to privately write down their responses to these three questions: 1) Which individual do you think will answer questions quickly and accurately? 2) Which of the two volunteers do you think is most similar to you? and 3) On a scale of one to ten, with ten being the highest, how well do you think YOU would perform on this task of mentally calculating multiple digit numbers?

The teachers were asked to flip over their paper, and the two volunteers stood up to begin. The rules were simple: I would show a calculation on the interactive white board, and the first person to answer the question accurately received a point. The problems started out simple (6+8 and 12+4) and grew to be a bit more complex (26+59, 84+77).

After the first five questions, the feeling in the room shifted. Teachers leaned forward in their seats, and my volunteers began more intently focusing on the board for the next question, shifting balance between their feet in quiet anticipation. After about ten questions, I stopped and asked the folks in their seats to answer one question now that they had seen the actual task: On a scale of one to ten, with ten, being the highest, how do you think that YOU would have performed in this same task?

Once everyone had written down their response to the final question, I asked everyone to take the number they had written down *before* the experience and subtract it from the number they had written down *after* the experience. Without asking folks to disclose their perceived ability, I asked for a show of hands in response to three different questions: 1) How many individuals had a positive number (e.g., their "after" number was higher than their "before" number); 2) How many individuals had a zero (e.g., their beliefs about their ability did not change before and after); and 3) How many individuals had a negative number (e.g., their "after" number was lower than their "before" number).

How we believe we'll perform a task is likely based on our previous experience of doing that task, as well as how we relate to others who can and cannot do the task well. For instance, if I asked you how well you think you might perform an open-heart surgery, you will likely say "not so well" unless you are a cardiothoracic surgeon. However, if I asked you how well you might respond to the above mental math task, you may say "quite well," especially if you are comparing yourself to someone who has just completed the same task whom you believe has capabilities equivalent to your own!

NEURAL UNDERPINNINGS OF EFFICACY AND PERSPECTIVE

While self-efficacy is a powerful predictor of our behavior and the risks we're willing to take in learning new information and more actively navigating rules in our environment, the discovery of the mighty neuron takes this work an exciting step further. In Chapter 1, we talked about neurons, those special cells in our brains that sends signals to activate a host of behaviors in our bodies. Included among these is the *mirror neuron*, which is a type of neuron especially attuned to this idea of collective rule creation.

The mirror neuron is a neural cell that fires when an individual acts on the world around them. But interestingly, this special cell not only fires when the individual acts but also when an individual sees *another* act. Some researchers have posited mirror neurons to be the neural foundation for perspective taking.[26] The discovery and ongoing research around the impact of mirror neurons suggest that each of us has neural foundations primed for the sole purpose of taking the perspective of others.[27]

Each new study showing the rich neural networks activated through playful experiences adds to the libraries of research educators can access that support more authentic and applied learning through play. As our neurons grow axons and dendrites to connect and send messages through synapses to other cells, they are continuously honed through experience.[28] The incredible neural resilience in the way our synapses fire to recreate ever-evolving networks of knowledge provides a rich landscape to explore and enhance the way we all learn and grow. The verbal, physical, and emotional navigation required to co-create during play solidifies these networks. When establishing shared rules, students are flexibly adapting what they know to acquire new information while actively moving and engaging with others. My belief is that play, or rich experiences embedded with opportunities to struggle and succeed together toward a shared goal, is what may best leverage our innate humanness to take on the most complex and exciting roles in our future.

IN IT TO WIN IT

The science of learning is embedded in the shared rules developed during game play. Together with the list of games your students help create in Level Up 4, it's important to think about the mode of the game. The modality of game play includes not only the platform (e.g., board game or digital simulation) but also the type of game play (e.g., collaborative, racing, battle royale, or role-playing games).

What is the purpose of game play and how are players challenged differently depending on the nature of the game? Unpacking the nature of your students shared experience during their "time off" helps you learn more about the unique learners in your class, including their interests and ways to connect on a deeper level.

The rules students naturally create or revise during a game are foundational to play. But rules are not simply for the sake of creating boundaries in the game. The boundaries that we create during play also allow players to come to shared agreements. But even the term *shared agreement* can get sticky if those agreements are not truly created together in a way that is as malleable as the games played on the schoolyard.

As educators we often use the term *rules* in application to a code of conduct or a prescriptive list of contracts we make in the classroom. The rules are meant to enforce compliance and don't always encourage creativity. Sure, the rules are there to keep our kids safe, but how many rules are there to support our kids in taking risks, being wrong, and bolstering one another in revising our learning? Moreover, how many of our rules are inclusive of both students and teachers? Who are the rules really serving?

In contrast, rules in games are shared agreements that help us thrive. In a game, the rules tell us the process for playing with an eye toward collaboration. Rules in classrooms, on the other hand, are often aimed at preserving individual conduct. The difference is that the asset-based approach of games reinforces the support and scaffolds for creativity and collaboration, whereas the deficit-based nature of many classroom rules traditionally focuses on conformity and compliance.

When students establish or are invited to reflect upon and update the rules, it not only helps guide game play but gives students a voice in an otherwise closed-door meeting. The process also provides a rich template for talking with students about who holds the keys to the game, what voices are loudest in establishing those roles, and how those roles are reinforced in our shared spaces.

READY TO PASS GO?

As we navigate the parameters of play, we are learning to navigate the parameters of our lives. Our rules of engagement are more rules *for* engagement, for building shared trust with those around us in order to live more connected lives, to build a sense of trust and perhaps empathy for one another, and if we're lucky, to help us to find ways to meaningfully contribute to our world in an effort to leave it better than we found it.[29]

In short, in defining our rules of engagement, we're developing powerful bonds to those around us and building the foundations for more empowered learning. This is learning that does not punish a mistake or limit your ability to move forward a grade with your peers; this is learning that ensures all our children get what they need to move forward together.

As we navigate the parameters of how we live, love, and work, we also find ways to connect with those around us and, in the process, learn more about who we are as individuals. What matters most to us today is different from what will matter most to us tomorrow, and engaging in dialogue about the parameters of what we will accept in our lives today shapes how we will change the world tomorrow.

Cognitive science continues to build support for what we know to be ideal environments for learning. Studies show how neural networks are activated through experience, revision, and continued effort, making game play a rich landscape to explore and enhance the way we all learn and grow. As children navigate the parameters of play, they are acquiring essential skills to make sense of multiple perspectives and viewpoints and to flexibly adapt to the world around them. They are also learning to trust their peers, their teachers, and other adults. Ultimately, they are learning how to build the future in which they most wish to live.

A HERO'S JOURNEY

I t's a mere three hours before dusk when a team of six researchers finally sets foot on the coast of the Marshall Islands in the central Pacific Ocean. The researchers are searching for samples of an indigenous leaf-footed bug (*Riptortus saileri*), a member of the Riptortus family of insects. These insects are known for cultivating healthy bacteria in their hosts and offer a glimmer of hope for better understanding our own human immune systems and the symbiotic relationships critical to our health.

With two significant factors working against them—flooding and radiation—the researchers must work quickly to seek out these specimens. Because it's the rainy season, much of the island is flooded and impossible to traverse. New research has found that, as the site of nearly seventy nuclear tests conducted by the US government in the late 1940s and '50s, the island may pose an even higher radiation threat than previously believed.

The six experts who arrive at the small islands, called atolls, are at the top of their respective fields. They include a diver, who is on standby due to the current threat of flooding; a pilot prepared to maneuver over rough terrain to support a quick departure; an engineer ready to determine the structural integrity of the collection site itself; a navigator intimately familiar with the region; a local who translates and facilitates communication among the researchers; and an entomologist-explorer whose research hinges on the discovery of this promising species.

Each expert has a role to play in safely collecting the samples and returning to the US mainland. Together they work quickly while the tide comes in, turning parts of the small island into a peninsula. Just as dusk turns to dark, the entomologist signals that she's found five samples, and the messenger calls ahead to the pilot to meet the team at the north edge of the island. The engineer determines the path is unsafe, as the influx of water has created a peninsula that now separates the engineer, navigator, and the diver from the others.

With a growing section of the land now completely submerged, the navigator suggests an alternate route based on a series of mathematical calculations. This will require the diver to move against the incoming tide to alert the others, while the navigator and engineer take the alternate route and hope for the best.

The pilot hears a whirring, or perhaps a siren, in the distance. This is strange, as they're inland, in the dark, and there is no sign of others within a hundred-mile radius. The sirens continue to blare, when suddenly the messenger announces, "We're late for gym guys. Let's leave Forbidden Island and finish when we get back."

As it turns out, we're not really in the Marshall Islands. Instead, we're in the back of a sixth-grade social studies classroom where students are playing a modified version of the commercial game Forbidden Island. They have taken on roles of various experts to learn about the topography of the remote Marshall Islands, the history of their people, the role of the United States in the islands' complex history, and the indigenous plants and animals that call these islands home.

THE DRIVE TO LEARN

Taking on roles to practice new knowledge and develop a sense of competence and autonomy is inherent in play. Doing so among others gives us a sense of relatedness and deepens purpose as we apply our skills. The games we play tell us not only *how* we learn best but also how we choose to *engage* with the world around us.

While the six players in the vignette that opened this chapter were not actually *on* the Marshall Islands, they *were* applying the knowledge needed to solve an important problem in the world around them today. Making tough choices, collaborating with others, and revising strategies after unexpected setbacks were all part of the process. What these students demonstrated in the span of a forty-five-minute class period are skills that will take them beyond the barriers of a standardized test and solidly into the active application of learning today.

So what is it about play that taps into our innate desire to engage with others and learn? Using the lens of motivation, cognitive science suggests some answers. Having already taken a look at the nature of learning, the potential of games, and the rules that set the stage for game play, in this chapter we turn to the individual student players to understand the essential components that invite expression of self during game play. Level Up 8 challenges you to keep an eye on learners as they identify the context for their learning as heroes of their journey. Through game play, we can explore how students respond to failure, how they explain their success, and even how learners identify the unique affordances of their learning.

LEVEL UP 8
A Hero's Journey

- How do the affordances of each hero's experience impact their journey (e.g., their caregivers, teachers, access to information)?
- When heroes fail, how do they move forward to become a stronger hero (e.g., seeking support, leaning on each other, asking questions)?
- When heroes succeed, how do they explain their success and the role of others in their learning journey?

From Playing to Making the Game

When people are engaged in activities for the sheer purpose of the activity and not for some external outcome, they are intrinsically motivated. When satisfaction is inherent in the task and not in some external reward, we are inclined to work harder toward a solution and feel purposeful in our efforts. This is a key distinction between intrinsic and extrinsic motivation and an essential understanding fundamental to the power of play.

Taking a step beyond simple intrinsic and extrinsic motivation we find self-determination theory, which describes three innate needs that motivate individuals: *competence*, *autonomy*, and *relatedness* (CAR for short).[30] When applied to learning this means that the individual must have a sense of competence in their knowledge, a voice and a choice in demonstrating how that knowledge is shared, and awareness of how the demonstration of knowledge makes them feel connected to others. This theory is specifically useful in understanding why our students may or may not choose to actively engage in learning.

This internal drive to contribute meaningfully to the world around us is how we flex our uniquely human capacity to be both creative and complex. Using a modified version of the commercial game Forbidden Planet, the previously highlighted students learned rich social studies, math, and science content while also actively engaging with one another.

In thinking about the engineer, navigator, diver, pilot, messenger, and explorer roles in the game, it becomes clear that the ownership each learner holds in playing Forbidden Island may itself be intrinsically motivating. A student who once claimed to dislike working on teams is now a navigator and master cartographer reading directions that will guide the others to safety. Similarly, a student who once wanted nothing to do with bugs is now an expert entomologist and can differentiate between an indigenous leaf-footed bug and a garden pest in their small New England town. Each student has an area of expertise they are contributing in collaboration toward a shared goal: collecting a sample of the correct species and evacuating the island before it is submerged.

In Forbidden Planet, as in many other games, taking on the role of "other" lowers the stakes for failure and allows players to more easily move outside of their comfort zones. The magic here is that in seeing the "other" succeed, you see yourself succeeding, too. Herein is the impetus for the intrinsically motivating factors of play, where the players see themself overcoming obstacles.

If the keys to each of our CARs include the ability to show what we know (competence) in a way that we choose (autonomy) by connecting with others (relatedness), then play is a powerful template for boosting intrinsic motivation. When students hold the keys to their own CAR, the sky's the limit.

Level Up 9 invites you to give students the keys to their own CAR while building off of the list constructed in Level Up 4 of games your students already play (*Fortnite* anyone?), as well as games you're likely quite comfortable with (please pass the tic-tac-toe!).

LEVEL UP 9
KEYS TO THE CAR

Use the list of games your students play (autonomy) to
- Invite groups of students to recreate those games (competence) with new content and rules, and
- Ask your students to share their newly created experiences with peers (relatedness).

The directives in Level Up 9 come straight from theories of motivation and invite us to think about how and where our students can show their brilliance, connect with others, and feel efficacious in their learning journey by bringing what they love into the four walls of the classroom.

During game play each player develops their sense of self and shares their growing expertise with peers. But a student's role as the hero on their journey is not limited to a classroom. In fact, game play can be used to deepen content knowledge and serve as a launching point for students to contribute meaningfully to the world today.

As teachers we can use motivational theories of learning to place students as the hero in their own journey. Edward Deci and Richard Ryan's work on self-determination is foundational to ensuring each of us is intrinsically driven in our lives. Yet my take on self-determination is that the keys to the CAR are even better suited to classroom learning when discussed as choice, voice, and community.

While classrooms provide a space for guided inquiry, they also house the potential for amplifying student voices in a safe space. By providing opportunities for students to explore flexible choices and develop a culture of learning through collaboration, we help students grow to become more adept citizens of the world, starting in their school and local community. What's more, by riffing on existing games using the content from your class, students are developing expertise and creativity.

LET THEM TAKE THE WHEEL

If the power of play is that it is low stakes, iterative, and collaborative, the power of our students as creators of their own playful learning is that together they form a safe community in which they can flex their choice and voice. When the script is flipped so that students are put in the driver's seat and help design their own learning, they develop a feeling of efficacy, and their motivation for learning moves from extrinsic to intrinsic. This is exciting stuff!

Locus of control is a fancy term for how people *perceive* others to play a role in their ability. When a student blames a teacher for a failing grade, the student places the blame outside themselves, whereas when that student sees that they did not submit the assigned project on time, the locus of control is internal. But it's not that simple. What if the child did not understand the assignment, was absent on the day it was explained, or simply did not know the right questions to ask to complete the assignment?

By leveraging the low-stakes and recursive nature of games and thus inviting students to take the wheel of learning, our students demonstrate knowledge and move that locus to internal control. Motivational research shows that students who hold an internal locus of control are more persistent. Our potential as skillful educators is to support students in seeing themselves as heroes in their journey. Our learners are then more likely to take on new and more challenging tasks and find ways to demonstrate their budding expertise in authentic ways well beyond the confines of a multiple-choice test.

Herein lies the potential of games to translate rote practice into the applied use of foundational learning, thus empowering students with the skills they need to succeed in the world around them. Every game has what are called mechanics, which drive how the game is played. You can use the game-play mechanics in Forbidden Planet to create a game about history of science where players take on new roles with a new mission that aligns to learning about sequencing the human genome.

Similarly, you could use those same game mechanics to teach about science throughout history, with a focus on the different scientists and technologies preceding thin-layer chromatography. The only question now: are your students truly invited to become heroes of their own journey?

In the introductory chapter we talked about the distinction between equality, equity, and the ultimate goal of justice. This is an important conversation to have in every space, and games provide a perfect platform to experience how powerful those distinctions are. When students are given permission to be the heroes in their own journey, they are empowered to modify games and find new, creative ways to play, allowing them to experience ownership, collaboration, and divergent thinking. Modifying games can be a powerful way for students to extend their knowledge and enhance all those rich neural networks of content knowledge in a playful but pointed area of study.

Using three well-known games as examples, Level Up 10 shows how games can be hacked to broaden their impact in your classroom. In hacking these particular games, your students will explore the systems at play in our world and come to see how not all economies are equitable for all, learn that not all causal relationships are positive, and discover that literary tropes are actually a mirror of the systems in which each character emerged.

LEVEL UP 10 CONSUMER TO CREATOR		
Game	**Potential Skills**	**Hack It**
Monopoly	Macro/microeconomics, inflation, taxes, prices, creation of money/resources	Equity: Collaborate to create new rules and spaces on the board to foster more equitable game play using landmarks from your town.
Apples to Apples	Associations, categories, vocabulary, perspective taking, parts of speech, cause and effect	Cause/Effect: Design a game where category and phrase cards match up to demonstrate causal relationships in the history of science.
Uno	Groups, colors, letters, numbers, operations (math), tropes (characters, figures of speech, imagery, themes)	Literary tropes: Recreate Uno with characters from your favorite texts across time, age, and theme, and reinvent the rules with flexible groupings (e.g., theme of the book, character traits).

To modify games, students simply use the mechanics or methods of game play from a familiar game and map on the content you're learning in class to create a whole new game. See if you can gain XP in Level Up 10 by adding ways your students can repurpose other beloved games to teach the content in your class. The excitement is palpable when students work in centers to play one another's games while also learning about everything from ancient Greece to elements on the periodic table.

Students become heroes in their own journey when an off-the-shelf game like Forbidden Planet is modified to apply content in a sixth-grade social studies class. So, too, can a favorite game of Uno be repurposed to teach taxonomy, fractions, or even central themes from great literary fiction. Working with teachers and students across the country, I've seen firsthand how modifying online games like *Minecraft* invites better understanding of ancient civilizations, and how reworking the rules of a simple card game like War helps primary-school students determine which words have more syllables than others!

Designing Each Hero's Journey

Cat is a curious seventh-grade student who wants to know everything about everything. Using a modified version of the dynamic simulation game Model Diplomacy, her social studies teacher helps students see themselves in the history of the world, making events from centuries past feel as current as the movements of today. This game comes complete with case notes on global issues, which provide background for students and prepare them to role play in an attempt to avert a global crisis.

In Cat's social studies class, her teacher has modified the game, which can be played throughout an entire semester or during a single class period. Each learner has a role to play and is guided by a series of salient articles that lay out the case. The game simulates a global environment where the economic, political, and social imperatives of each nation impact one another. And what's more, the simulation is led entirely by students.

Intrinsically motivated to engage in game play, Cat leads a group of students to consider the moral implications of sabotaging their sister nation. Students lose track of time while immersed in debate about the economic repercussions of not overthrowing their sister nation to access hidden oil reserves.

Through this free simulation game, each student's voice is raised to contribute their unique perspective on a global issue. Together, students are asked to consider multiple perspectives of their actions: environmental crises, economic potential, ethnic tensions, the potential of food scarcity. Together they design their story and try on roles they may one day hold as leaders in a new global economy.

During game play, each player develops a sense of self and shares their brilliance with the world. As you think about the list of games you and your students know and love, consider the power of bringing those experiences into the classroom to encourage your learners' voices and choices while developing the community. Reflect on how, while engaging in playful experiences into the classroom, your students are sharing and recreating experiences with their peers. Which games are easily modified and which ones need a little extra time to rebuild?

ME TO WE: RENAMING THE GAME

Connecting the hero's journey to the six experts playing a modified version of Forbidden Island, I can see clearly that we may be asking the wrong questions in much of our current debate in education. What if, instead of debating the utility of homework, we ask about the impact of practice versus application? Once a child knows his times tables, what is the utility of practicing an entire sheet of times tables? As an educator, I believe it's preferable to use those skills to solve actual problems. In fact, the critical thinking and applied content knowledge required to calculate how many feet one has until they reach the flooded zone or how much gas a pilot needs to safely traverse the Pacific Ocean to return six weary experts home feels much more practical than a worksheet of fractions.

Or what about, in a riff on the beloved games of Spoons, you have students repurpose a deck of cards to create elements from the periodic table? Instead of collecting four of a kind as they would in Spoons, they can challenge one another to create chemical compounds. In this game, which I created with learners and called EleMental, players have fun with their classmates while demonstrating their understanding of ionic, covalent, and metallic bonds.

Whether playing a modified version of an off-the-shelf game or creating their own game, students become heroes of their own learning experience while taking on roles as leaders, citizens, and collaborators. Students feel a sense of efficacy in sharing something deeply personal and potentially profound with their peers. They will demonstrate competence in content to recreate a beloved game with their knowledge, in autonomy in how they demonstrate that knowledge, and in relatedness in sharing this new experience with peers.

Longtime education writer and author of the book *The Game Believes in You: How Digital Play Can Make Our Kids Smarter*, Greg Toppo believes there are seven reasons why games bring out the very best in each of us. In fact, all seven are words that begin with the letter F—perhaps the first time an entire list of F words is appropriate for use in school! The words—failure, feedback, fairness, flow, fantasy, freedom, and fellowship—align beautifully with the research in cognitive science that shows how we learn best.

Cognitive science demonstrates the power of the intrinsic motivation necessary to support learners in being heroes of their own journey. This research provides insights into how this knowledge can be applied to level up learning each day. Skillful educators are essential for guiding students through engaged learning experiences, and self-determination is the intrinsic motivator to keep students in the game.[31]

Perhaps the key to engaged learning is in ensuring our students acquire foundational knowledge to succeed. However, this must be in combination with the essential and malleable skills of communication, collaboration, critical thinking, and creativity, which will prepare our students for an exciting and uncertain future.

While there is no single unifying theory for a neurobiological foundation of intrinsic motivation, much of the research suggests the intersection of thinking (cognitive), acting (behavioral), and reg-ulating (social-emotional) action are all essential ingredients. In contrast to reductionist views of learning that look specifically at one contributing factor, neurobiological research is reinforcing more of a constructivist view, in which there are many factors at play in supporting students in learning. In fact, neurobiolog-ical research is reinforcing what educators have known for quite some time: students must have choice, voice, and connection to content to want to learn. Games provide exactly this.

YOU HAVE TO FREE A LOT OF FROGS: LESSONS LEARNED FROM FROGGER

Jonathan was an articulate and passionate communicator in my classroom. He never shied away from a conversation and was always ready to lead, whether it was a game of wall ball or the singing of the latest silly camp song I'd shared with them as we prepared for the daily math lesson. Luckily for me, I taught math after lunch, so I had an entire period before the kids returned to prepare manipulatives a lesson in equivalent fractions one day.

Jonathan was also the first to entertain my idea of an entry activity—a choice to share a dance move, make a silly face, or recite a silly sentence before entering the classroom. On this day, he did a compelling rendition of the cha-cha slide. This child was remarkable in his ability to put kids at ease and make anything feel possible. At least that was the case until he realized that a math "do now" was on the board: What is an equivalent fraction for 1/4? Sucking teeth, he quickly found his seat and hunkered down in silent resignation.

The children took a few minutes to jot down their thoughts in their notebooks, and then shared their equivalent fractions with one another. The noise level in the classroom was neither very high nor very low, but the general feeling of malaise was unmistakable. In a moment of desperation, I ditched the day's lesson and called everyone to the rug.

I asked my kids, "Who played wall ball today and who played jump rope?" My students shared that seven of the twenty-six kiddos in the class had played wall ball and fourteen had jumped rope. (Five kids were absent.) They laughed as I drew seven stick figures holding handballs. Then I drew a line below the seven stick figures playing wall ball and beneath the line I drew twenty-six faces with giant Us for jump ropes.

"Seven over twenty-six. Is this a fraction?" I asked.

"Yes!" They agreed.

"What if we only had six friends in the class and three jumped rope?" I asked.

Jonathan raised his hand. "There would be three of our funny stick people jumping rope with a line and six faces below."

When I asked if he'd like to try, Jonathan proudly walked to the chart paper and drew three stick figures with giant Us for jump ropes underneath. He then penned a solid line beneath all three jump ropers. He completed his drawing with six simple smiley faces drawn just underneath the line. Jonathan stepped away, looked at his work, and beamed with pride.

I asked, "So what would that look like as a fraction?"

He quickly drew the corresponding 3/6 fraction. "Piece of cake!" he beamed.

As he returned to the rug, I asked the children, "What would be another way of showing the same *value* with different numbers? What number goes into both the top and bottom number?" A sea of hands raised high, and Alice said, "There would be a one on the top and a three on the bottom."

I asked if all my kids agreed, and they nodded vigorously. I then grabbed a stack of index cards and placed my kids in groups of two. Each group received four index cards, one card where I had written one of four fractions (e.g., 1/2 , 1/3, 1/4, or 1/5), and three other cards where they had to write and then draw an equivalent fraction.

My kiddos quickly got to work, and after seven minutes of creating, they had four different cards representing the fractions 1/2, 1/3, 1/4, and 1/5. Placing all the fraction cards I had created with a simple fraction (e.g., 1/2 , 1/3, 1/4, or 1/5) in one pile, the students now put the equivalent fraction cards (the ones they had created with pictures to match the 1/2 , 1/3, 1/4, or 1/5) cards in a separate pile. I placed students into groups of four and said, "*You* just made a game. Ready to play?"

Knowing my tendency toward shenanigans, they nodded cautiously but with great interest, and I introduced the game. "Everyone gets three of the picture-with-fraction cards. These are the equivalent, or answer, cards. The plain fraction cards stay face down in the center of the table. *Capisce?*" There was more nodding.

"The goal is to get rid of your equivalent cards first. The way you do that is by matching your equivalent fraction card to the fraction card in the middle. One person flips over the plain fraction card, and the first person to place their correct equivalent fraction card atop the plain fraction card wins. The first person to get rid of all their equivalent fraction cards wins the whole game."

"Are you ready to play?" I ask.

The children answer with a resounding yes, grabbing their piles of cards and scurrying back to their tables. The room quickly filled with boisterous giggles as the children decided who would be first in placing their card down. Soon the kids were adding rules for what to do when there was a tie: the first person to share another equivalent fraction broke the tie and won. And guess who came up with that rule after being one of the children to tie in placing their cards? You guessed it—Jonathan.

Reframing Setbacks as Success in Progress

Every time your kid sister outscores you at Scrabble or your child narrowly misses a Victory Royale in *Fortnite*, there is valuable learning embedded in that setback. The power of play as a captivating means for engaging learners is well-founded in learning research. But what makes play even more powerful as a means of learning is the fact that during play, failure is seen as feedback or as fuel for future learning.

Current trends in education seem to be focused on what often feels like bootstrapping persistence. If only our students "pressed on" or "tried harder," they would all ace that exam. What is missing is the context for this persistence, which can be quite detrimental to many of our learners. The grit to press on despite setbacks can be problematic for learners—or anyone—without adequate support. The idea itself raises significant issues of equity. For instance, what are we really measuring when we ask language learners to solve a mathematical problem written as a narrative (e.g., a story problem)?

What assumptions are we making when we place the onus on a student to press on instead of considering structural inequities that contribute to larger class sizes, underfunded classrooms, and implicit bias that privileges some learners and is detrimental to others? Perhaps it's time to check our assumptions of what it means to be successful and the opportunities students really need to experience mastery. The task of creating more intrinsically motivated learners requires each of us to take a hard look in the mirror and acknowledge the latent biases that may prevent us from seeing students as already filled with the "grit" that is supposed to solve all their problems.

Take a moment and watch a kid play *Minecraft*. See them get beaten by the Ender Dragon, then hop right back into another game of *Minecraft* without a second thought. The idea of mindset is nice, but unless kids care about the work, it's a struggle. How can we embed meaningful experiences into learning so there's a desire to persist against the odds?

Observing students at play serves a dual purpose: understanding not only the risks they are willing to take but also *how* they are willing to take those risks. These observations provide nuggets of insight that make research come to life. On the one hand, games model how to create an environment where learners feel supported in taking risks. On the other hand, they show *how* our students are motivated from within to respawn and try again even if they are unsuccessful.

In the opening vignette, my bright student, Jonathan, was uninspired to do yet another math task. When reducing fractions turned into a group activity with low stakes that was built around conversation and collaboration, he eagerly joined in. When we co-created a game that felt similar to Uno, it was all the more accessible for Jonathan and the twenty-five other students. By reframing the lesson to something both tangible and revelant, they were ready to become experts in fractions.

Of course, games alone are not a panacea for the access to support all learners need to find success. Yet there are lessons to be learned in looking deeply at the nature of games and more closely at play. They can show us how and why we are more likely to persist despite fear of failure. What is it embedded within play that encourages us to keep trying?

PLAY: REFRAMING FAILURE AS THE PROCESS OF LEARNING

For many years, the word *play* has been relegated to the ballfields or the schoolyard. This push has been even more severe as a response to the demand for a more academically rigorous curriculum has grown. But those of us who have played or watched our children play ball know that the ability to brush yourself off after a foul and get back into the game is a coveted and significant skill.

The emergence of e-sports is giving even more children the opportunity to engage in this learning process. In fact, the e-sports landscape demonstrates the application of learning science. In the summer of 2019, the *Fortnite* World Cup, an event celebrating one of the most popular digital games around, was held. Over two million people worldwide streamed the finals live—including my own children and likely even your own!

Because electronic sports take place on a digital platform, they are embedded with communication mechanisms between players. It's only natural then for our children to follow the players' social media feeds. On May 4, 2019, the player Reverse2K shared a profound tweet on social media that resonated not only with me as an educator but also with my kids, who are serious gamers: *So 77 points today with my boy @Ninja. We made some dumb mistakes but fixed them for tomorrow!* This was a powerful message: even our stars see failure as the process of learning.

Reframing failure as feedback for learning is not novel to educators or professionals at any level, but the digital revolution that ushered in a new age of access to those at the top of their game helps our students see that intentional and flexible practice is the key to developing skills in any domain. In a single social media message, our children hear what famed psychologist Anders Ericsson has been saying for decades: expertise is honed over decades of intense and focused practice.[32] What our kids see is that with a clear idea of what needs improving, you have a plan for moving forward.

It is not simply that one must follow the rule of ten years or ten thousand hours to be an expert, but that certain skills can be learned through intentional play. Our role in education is in highlighting opportunities for growth that are meaningful to our learners so they can hone their own unique expertise.

A recent study from Ericsson's lab looked at the use of a verbal protocol when training players to improve their score during game play.[33] Not surprisingly, with a more knowledgeable other to provide just-in-time scaffolds, players are more successful. In terms of education, this reinforces the "guide-on-the-side" approach championed by Vygotsky.[34] As guides on the side, expert teachers allow students to share how they understand the world around them. The student's explanations may take many forms, but the goal is to place the learner at the center and honor the process of acquiring knowledge. Interestingly enough, this is similar to the strategies used by cognitive scientists looking to make knowledge visible. . . er . . .audible! Using think-aloud protocols allows learning scientists to study the nature of knowledge and knowing, especially when making decisions during learning. In Level Up 11 you'll find questions that will demonstrate just how persistent your students already are while celebrating the hard, but exciting, process of trial and error.

LEVEL UP 11
REFOCUS ON THE PROCESS

- Where did you trip up?
- How did you feel getting back in the game?
- Who was there to help you?
- What did you try differently the second (third, fourth, or more) time?
- What's your new goal *this* time?

While parents, teachers, peers, and many others can serve as a knowledgeable other, in the digital age a more knowledgeable other can even be a ninja. Don't believe me? Hop on to a computer and go to YouTube. Once there do a search for ninja and *Minecraft*. Go ahead, I'll wait. What you'll find is an abundance of videos of gamers talking their way through game play. This is a modern-day take on the think-aloud strategies used by master teachers. Whether helping an elementary-school student contextualize reading or a college-aged student hold multiple perspectives, this is what teachers do best.

While our students actively choose to play *Minecraft* or *Fortnite* in their free time at home, many educators are bringing these experiences to the classroom. Those who are embracing this new way to play are finding some surprisingly impressive benefits. Researchers Tisha Ellison and Jessica Evans followed Jim Pike, a third-grade teacher who used *Minecraft* to create an entire curriculum called *Mathcraft*, aligned to his mathematics curriculum.[35] They found that students using the hallmark blocks of *Minecraft* learned algebra and increased their math scores 66 percent in a single school year!

Caveat: Sadly for me, I am not at all affiliated with *Minecraft*. I simply find it to be one of the most brilliant ways teachers are leveraging the technologies our students crave and inventing opportunities to move beyond consumption and into the creation that invites students into the process of learning. These digital sandbox games foster the skills we most want to see in our learners—the ability to reflect on their learning in a safe and ongoing way.

As educational psychologist Lee Shulman and his mentees understand, a teacher's unique magic lies at the intersection of their content knowledge and their knowledge of teaching (Shulman termed this intersection *pedagogical content knowledge*).[36] This is where empowered educators skillfully guide learners to reflect on their learning and plan, monitor, and assess how they'll iterate forward. It's also foundational to the skills of metacognition and self-regulated learning, which we'll also talk about in this chapter.

The affordances of playful learning through games may be a way to reframe the rally cry of "just try harder" to considering what supports seem to work for different learners. In doing so, we can help each learner feel accomplished in our classrooms. The questions in Level Up 12 can be shared with students or used as reflection points for savvy educators seeking out the Goldilocks zone within your classroom—the place where learning isn't too hard or too easy but is just right.

LEVEL UP 12
FAILURE IS SUCCESS IN PROGRESS

- What do you know?
- How can you show?
- Where can you grow?
- Who do you know that can help you to grow?

Answers to the questions in Level Up 12 will provide valuable insight into not only what each learner knows but also how they apply that learning. Making learning visible shows where this is room to grow and helps us see who else in the class our kids feel comfortable learning with to grow those dendrites!

THE ONLY FAILURE IS NOT LEARNING FROM MISTAKES

In Chapter 1, I shared the distinction between gamification and game-based learning. As the litmus for how a player progresses, a leaderboard is an important artifact of game play. Taken alone, however, the leaderboard reduces game play to the single output and ignores the beauty of the process. It is no different from behavior modification systems where kids move clothespins from green to yellow to red when their behavior is not compliant.

In essence, gamification takes the leaderboard of a game that shows where players are during game play and uses it as an extrinsic way to motivate students toward compliance. In contrast, the best use of game-based learning invites students to co-create and maintain their own leaderboards. The process of keeping track of their progress reinforces important skills of knowing when you know, or *metacognition*, a powerful cognitive tool to improve learning.

The skills of metacognition ask students to think about their thinking during the learning process. This ability helps students become self-regulated learners, whereby they learn to plan, monitor, and assess their own learning. Taken together, these skills are not a means to an end but the essential process for supporting students in taking charge of their own learning. These two fundamental components of cognition—metacognition and self-regulated learning—place the role of monitoring learning behavior in the hands of our students. No behavior chart necessary!

Putting students in the driver's seat of their own learning does not relegate teachers to the back seat but instead positions them as passengers. Think about learning how to drive. You likely spent many hours in cars as a passenger prior to sitting in the driver's seat for the very first time. The first time you took the wheel you already had a schema for what was supposed to happen and a framework for your role as the driver. Before students take the wheel, they need to have the example of a thoughtful and experienced educator. In her book *In Schools We Trust*, educator Deborah Meier reinforces the importance of our role as educators as empowerers and supporters as our children take on new and exciting challenges.[37]

To this end, I propose a new type of leaderboard. In this re-envisioned leaderboard, which may or may not have a physical manifestation, learning lives with the student. Instead of focusing on those who rise to the top or flop toward the bottom, the focus is on empowering and emboldening our children to embrace setbacks as opportunities to learn and to seek out their peers for clues and guidance in finding those well-hidden Easter eggs—hidden features of games that make play so deliciously exciting! This type of leaderboard celebrates the fact that the hundreds of shifts our kids make to their thinking daily to revise and rethink their work is where learning magic happens.

Level Up 13 presents one version of this leaderboard, where students share their learning journey, focusing on what they've mastered, where they're going, and what they've learned that they can share with others. The goal is to engage students in conversations about how they learn, where they struggle, where they shine, and how together they hold the key to solutions that may very well change the world!

LEVEL UP 13 **FAILURE IS SUCCESS IN PROGRESS**			
Player	**Challenge Mastered**	**Current Challenge to Master**	**Clues & Easter Eggs**
Jayden	Expert of __	Currently mastering __	A trick I can share is . . .
Grace	Expert of __	Currently mastering __	A secret I now know is. . .
Liam	Expert of __	Currently mastering __	A way to level up here is. . .
Ava	Expert of __	Currently mastering __	Something that blew my mind was. . .

USE IT OR LOSE IT

A rich literature exists around the impact of *distributed practice* in classroom learning. In the late 1880s psychologist Hermann Ebbinghaus noted that content not often recalled is likely to be lost. This prompted libraries of research, including that of Shana Carpenter, whose research lab has been hard at work to demonstrate the impact of regular applied practice on the retention of knowledge. Simply put, distributed practice is the antithesis of cramming for a test. Instead, consistent practice a little bit each day and over a period of time ensures that you're more likely to recall what you practice than if you cram it all into one session. While a few decades too late for my undergraduate career, this cautionary tale is an important message to learners and leaders hoping to support learners in not just knowing but growing their knowledge.

Distributed practice in classrooms supports students in becoming more proficient readers, writers, and communicators.[38] Distributed practice in game play happens organically as players continuously revisit and hone their skills while playing, and it is likely enhanced by playing alongside others. While it's true you can play games in solo mode, the joy is most evident when games are played with others. These connections not only strengthen neural pathways to enhance understanding but also grow more connected communities of learners.

It is not simply the choice of where to begin, how to collaborate with peers, and what skills to grow; intentional practice solidifies and grows knowledge. Game play is powerful because those skills are honed through intentional and repeated practices. Players continue to plan before play, play and fail, and then try again. Each individual is motivated to play again and again, learning from the mistakes they've made to improve next time while also supporting one another. All of this is of their own volition, with no sanctions or standardized test necessary. Imagine that! Isn't this exactly what we aspire to in our classrooms?

Distributed practice, where a little practice each day strengthens connections across our neural networks, helps us become more successful tomorrow than we were today. While the myth of the learning style persists, playful learning shows us that when students are driven by interest and opportunity, repeated play turns areas of passion turn into areas of expertise. For instance, in *Fortnite*, one player becomes the master builder and squad members trade building materials for supplies they need to enhance their own areas of interest and passion. Today it might just be a game of *Fortnite*, but tomorrow these same students may very well be engineering a more sustainable city.

USE THE FORCE

Our students are not the only ones continuously innovating on their work and working toward shared goals. As educators we can use our own superpowers to help colleagues level up their game, and we can call on the superpowers of others to improve our own game. In fact, the sample leaderboard in Level Up 13 is similar to what I use when running professional-development sessions and workshops across the country.

You may wish to try this simple process with your colleagues or even your digital professional learning network—or on Twitter, your #PLN— as a way to leverage your expertise across the globe and level up together through shared insights and goals. Collaborating with colleagues is like entering the warp zone in a game; you can exponentially increase your professional learning by connecting with others whose dreams and needs match your expertise and whose "shares" might be just what you've been seeking to bring to life in your classroom!

When working with educators, I ask three simple questions:

DREAMS: What is a pie-in-the-sky *dream* for your work this year in the classroom?
Sample answer: To have my students gamify three novels as choose-your-own-adventure stories.

NEEDS: What do you *need* to attain that goal?
Sample answer: A better understanding of role-playing games with high replay value, and to connect with colleagues who've done this before.

SHARES: What superpower do *you* have that your colleagues may not know about but that could be valuable to them?
Sample answer: Did you play Dungeons & Dragons or Euchre in college? Are you a certified scuba diver who could be a content expert for students in marine biology even though you teach ELA?

Just as our students amend and update their learning to move forward through scaffolded and ongoing guidance, so can we leverage the support of our colleagues and acknowledge our own ongoing learning. What a powerful model for our learners!

CREATION OVER CONSUMPTION

Taking tired content and turning it into a playful game together with my learners was an opportunity to practice those pesky fractions in a way that invited different types of skills from traditional math work. Learners were part of the creation, not simply consumers of prepopulated worksheets. What's more, they unknowingly created a game where the low-stakes nature of play invited discussion among peers and creative navigation of otherwise complicated concepts (to my second graders).

The experience of turning a tough concept into a game allowed for growth and progress to continue organically. Learning is not a linear process, and what this experience taught me was that inviting students to co-create experiences also helped my students overcome their uncertainty with different concepts. It made the abstract concrete. Moreover, it included others in the process of sharing those delightful-smelling Magic

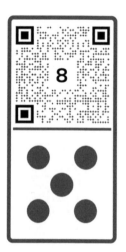

Markers with my young learners as together we creatively found a way to learn through play!

The name of the game in learning is creation over consumption. Beware gamified digital worksheets and instead invite students to become the co-creators of their own learning games and tools. In Chapter 5 we'll talk about the many ways working together through play enhances learning. Don't be afraid to join in as your students design, develop, and devise more playful ways of approaching learning together!

READY PLAYERS TWO, THREE, AND FOUR

It was one of the first really cold Sunday nights in November. The sun had set far too early and the ground was still wet from a flurry of snowy rain. My sons' soccer games had both been canceled because the fields were too wet to safely play, and the friends each boy had invited over to spend the day inside with had been picked up by their parents. Hunkering down in our living room around the first fire of the season, my oldest son, J, asked, "Can we play a round of squads?" He was asking to play a game of *Fortnite* in a squad, or group of four friends. They would work together to be the last team standing in hopes of achieving the holy grail of *Fortnite* playing, a Victory Royale!

After a day of watching movies while buried in blankets, my gut response to my eleven-year-old was no. But as I looked at his sweet little face all filled with hope and eager to play after a rained-out game, I questioned my reticence, realizing that a half hour wouldn't be that big of a deal. Before I could answer, he said, "But Mom, if we play, you have to promise to watch us, okay?" That sealed the deal, and soon my two boys were loading *Fortnite* onto our shared screen. In homes more than twenty minutes away from ours, their friends Z and C were doing the same.

There is a lot of debate over this game—enough, in fact, that when certain friends visit, we tell the kids not to play it for fear of causing unnecessary problems. But as I watched my youngest, L, put on his headset and start organizing his squad to play and heard my oldest not only agree but begin to work with him, I realized I was witnessing a powerful experience unfolding.

My little one spoke strongly into his microphone and asked, "Everybody ready up?" As if in lockstep, the oldest said, "Yep!" His response was followed by a "Yassss" and an "I'm in." Soon all four kids were engaged in a full-on conversation that turned into a complex negotiation as they determined where to drop and how they would approach play. My youngest son was transformed into a new person when I heard him say, "Why don't J and C start in Frenzy, and then Z and I can drop in Slurpy and meet you at Salty before the storm?"

The boys seemed to be in accord that this was a good plan. I watched as the teams headed in their respective directions. Together they searched for supplies, and they fashioned complicated structures to protect themselves from other squads as well as the storm raging around them. They navigated directions, made decisions about what their priorities were, addressed the team's needs, and negotiated with each other.

I made a mental note that this was more talking than I'd heard from them all day. Though I watched quietly at first, soon the researcher in me took over and I couldn't help but start asking questions. "What are you using to build that structure?" I asked my youngest. "I'm using wood," he explained, quickly adding, "There are three materials you can use: wood, brick, and metal. Wood starts out at a higher HP (health points) so I'm more protected." Apparently, this means that while the other two materials (brick and metal) are initially stronger, over time, the wood is most successful in withstanding an attack.

As I was talking with my youngest, my oldest chimed in to say, "Look Mom, this structure has 560 health now, but it was shot twice. Each shot was 70 damage, that's 140 points total. Now the health is at 420, but it will get stronger again fast. Just watch." Remarkably my children were not only registering my presence but were also responding to my curiosity with details that happened to include mental math. Fascinating.

In the end, I couldn't keep track of much of the action as my sons were playing on parallel screens, but I do know that they eventually get the coveted "dub," or the win, and excitedly celebrated together for a moment before beginning another game.

YOU CAN'T WIN IF YOU DON'T (LEARN THROUGH) PLAY

There is much to be admired in the design of a good game. Well-designed games and other playful experiences seem to have in spades exactly what educational policies often miss by wide margins: interdisciplinary collaboration toward a shared goal.

In well-designed experiences, the playing is the learning. Take for example, the way orientation and navigation are handled in *Fortnite*. In this game, players are literally dropped into play with a twenty-thousand-foot view mapping the entire game space. This allows players to get oriented to the spaces and places before they begin game play. This is in lieu of a complicated map that requires toggling between screens in digital games or the often-convoluted paper map in more traditional games that, at least in my house, is usually lost after the second or third time playing.

During game play, a sense of where locations are in relation to one another helps players successfully navigate and communicate in their shared space. Understanding cardinal directions is inherent in playing the game and is not the end but the means to the end. This is distinct from traditional modes of learning in which discrete skills are taught ad nauseum, siloed from their actual use.

However, it's not the map alone, or even the math involved in determining how much health is remaining or how to trade materials, that makes *Fortnite* praiseworthy. The kids were also connecting and supporting one another during the game. I watched as one player healed a teammate while another built a structure to protect them from incoming squads. The cooperation, communication, creativity, and critical thinking that is embedded within the game play activates a deeper connection to content and to one another in the multiplayer experience. Navigating one's way through the multiplayer experience in *Fortnite* requires collaboration, which helps us take the perspective of others and may ultimately lead to empathy.

Watching children discuss strategy, do math on the fly, and talk about cardinal directions in the context of a game strikes me as the very best potential classroom experience. In squads, players work together toward a shared goal, each with their unique abilities. Though different kids get excited and interested in specializing in different skills, those who are masterful in one area may teach those who are less masterful in that same domain. Importantly, it is the opportunity for each player to grow their skills through collaboration with peers that gives playful learning a more low-stakes feel and supports creativity and risk taking. Moreover, it is the collaborative engagement toward a shared goal that makes playful learning powerful and enjoyable.

Better Together: Playful Learning for Collaborative Learning

In the playful experience at the beginning of this chapter, the motivational theory of self-determination is evident. Individual players may choose where they'd like to begin game play, developing their sense of autonomy. Players choose what skills they will hone, developing a sense of competence. Lastly, players identify where they need support and how they will seek out team members to achieve ultimate success, contributing to a strong sense of relatedness to others in their shared space.

What we see in games is the power of self-determined motivation and the importance of the other players in the space.[39] Players are motivated to play the same game multiple times. This repeated game play allows them to learn from mistakes made together. Moreover, these lessons show players how to support and help one another move forward.

According to famed social psychologist Albert Bandura, we learn not only by the actions we take and by observing the actions of others, but also from how we see ourselves compared to the models around us. In addition, we are often more likely to internalize what we have learned in this way if we also identify strongly with the individual we are observing. Social learning theorists know that oftentimes the best road to learning is through social modeling, similar to how we all learn through play.

If you take a minute to observe a group of kids at recess, you'll see some of this powerful social learning in practice. You may notice children in one corner negotiating rules during a game of boxball. In another space you may see a group of kids organizing a pick-up game of soccer. In each instance you're likely to see similar connections to social learning and scaffolds like we saw in the opening vignette. Game play is a team sport.

But the collaboration embedded in playful experiences is not only beneficial for learning to coordinate and work together, it's also an essential element for getting to know other people. Moreover, in learning more about others, you become open to hearing about the experiences of others to understand how your experiences are similar and distinct.

During playful learning and open play, not only are our children able to flex their autonomy, but they can also learn to take the perspective of their peers. If we're deliberate and intentional about including playful experiences during learning, the ways our students learn to take the perspective of others may also help them develop a greater sense of empathy. Is it possible that the nature of game play, in which we seek understanding and collaboration to grow, identify obstacles as setbacks, and find ways to thrive together, is the secret to success in life?

Playful learning is a low-stakes way to introduce perspective while putting your skills to practice. When Dorothy and friends followed the Yellow Brick Road to the Emerald City in *The Wizard of Oz*, it was implied that this road was a pathway to success if they stayed the course.

Just as Dorothy and her friends each had unique skills and hopes for their journey to Oz, so, too, do different students have different skills and hopes for learning during play.

What was unknown as Dorothy gathered her group was how critical each character's skills would be to the ultimate success of the journey. As they followed the Yellow Brick Road to the Emerald City, each friend grew the skills they needed for individual success, which led to the success of the group.

The magic of play is not just in the low-stakes and deliberate practice embedded within the nature of activity. During game play, learning and growth seem to happen simultaneously. The magic lies in the connection between humans that we all need to grow and thrive. Using the prompts from Level Up 14, you can identify which students may be interested in working with one another and help your learners find a common language to identify their uniquely valuable attributes and connect to their peers in a more meaningful and purposeful way.

LEVEL UP 14		
LEARNING THROUGH COLLABORATION		
Who are three people in the class that you work with regularly?	What is a quality about each of those people that you most admire?	
	How have each of their skills inspired you in some way?	
Who are three people in this class that you've never worked with?	What is one quality about each of these people that inspires you most?	
	What is one attribute of each of these people that you most admire?	

Just as the Yellow Brick Road brought Dorothy and her friends to the Emerald City, neural pathways, which are strengthened by engaging in repeated playful learning with others, lead our learners to success. The more these pathways are traversed, the more our understanding is secured. And the more these pathways connect to other pathways or information, the better they become reinforced and honed over time. This is the beauty of distributed practice: repeated play or growth over time that reinforces and enhances connections.

PRACTICE IN PLAY:
FROM PERSPECTIVE TO EMPATHY

Play is often a team sport and is thus a fertile breeding ground for collaboration and communication. But it is also a space where the cultivation and curation of new ideas emerge, and where we are encouraged to take the perspective of another person. Therefore, the ways we connect during play might plant the seeds of empathy.

The questions in Level Up 14 identify which students work together frequently and those who may benefit from a bit of a departure from the norm. If we ask our students to identify with whom they typically engage, we are likely to see who is getting left out and perhaps create a more inclusive classroom community. The neural underpinnings of learning are powerful, yet it is the social system in which they take place that reinforces and strengthens their connections.

What's more, as we learn by watching others play, the unique and mighty mirror neuron helps us understand the intention of the others with whom we are playing. This fascinating class of neurons has been the focus of many studies by researchers who believe they help humans understand the intention of other people's actions. It is not a stretch to suggest that while observing others in order to plan our next move in a game, our mirror neurons are activated. The low-stakes nature of play may be an ideal way to plant the seeds of empathy. With clear roles in game play, there is certainty (it's not your turn to roll the die), but there's no summative test that creates a sense of anxiety.

Let's look at the game Apples to Apples, a card game in which a judge flips over an adjective card (e.g., valuable) and players compete to contribute the noun card (e.g., toasted marshmallows, horses, or dishwashers) they believe the judge will deem the best fit. The game is based on each player's ability to guess what the judge will think. Yes, this game is wholly subjective. The point is that understanding the perspective of the player who is acting as the judge is often more important than selecting the card that you consider the best fit.

Is the judge an aspiring chef? In that case, toasted marshmallows may be truly valuable! Or is your judge someone whose chore is washing dishes after dinner? That judge may ascribe greater value to a dishwasher. The important concept here is that understanding the intentions of others is a useful skill. Whether it's teachers connecting with students or students connecting with their peers in a friendly match of Apples to Apples, those mighty mirror neurons are furiously firing to help us see ourselves in others and, if we're lucky, help us become more empathetic.

In Level Up 15 you'll find some simple prompts to use before, during, or after game play to scaffold conversations about how your students see one another and how they see themselves. With an eye toward social learning theory, we can discover not only how our students perceive others but also give our students a lens to take the perspective of their peers in new and potentially transformative ways. Celebrating the successes of others and identifying the divergent ways students approach solving similar problems is a powerful way to honor every student in the classroom.

LEVEL UP 15
PERSPECTIVE TAKING TOWARD EMPATHY

- When playing the game, what is an action a player took that most *surprised* you?
- How was their action *different* from the action you may have taken?
- What would *you* have done in that same position?
- *Why* did their action surprise you?
- Why do you *think* that person chose to take that action?
- Why do you think the person's action was *different* from what you expected?
- What is one *reason* they may have taken that action that you hadn't considered before?

SOWING THE SEEDS OF EMPATHY THROUGH PLAY

Across the life span, neurological changes, including the ability to regulate behavior, impact the way we interact with others and the way we learn. The ability to take the perspective of others, and in doing so gain a sense of empathy, is a particularly sweet spot for play, specifically because each player is naturally positioned in the seat of an "other" during play. Some researchers have even found that play changes the empathy-related neural networks of middle-school students.[40]

Seated in our amygdala is our ability to regulate emotion and affect. Some researchers have looked to the amygdala to see how play impacts our ability to process emotion and perhaps even regulate empathy. In an attempt to determine how different game play may impact the underlying cognitive structures connected to empathy in adolescent brains, researchers at the University of Wisconsin had middle-school students play one of two games.

The first game, Crystals, was created specifically for the study and required players to recognize the emotions of humanlike creatures. Players were supposed to attend to the facial expressions of these near-human others, as well as head movements and other very human behaviors, in order to guess their emotional states. The second game, Bastion, was a commercial game where players collect raw materials to save their village.

The researchers' interesting and impressive findings for the players who were asked to read emotional states from the faces of avatars was that engaging in this form of play qualitatively changed the structure of the players' neural networks. Specifically, researchers found neurological correlations with what they call empathetic accuracy in some of the players who played Crystals. This game was created specifically to induce perspective taking or empathy for the humanlike others, and it did just that.

The right *temporoparietal junction* is a region of the brain responsible for both cognitive (e.g., attention) and emotional (e.g., empathy) functions. This study found that this region functionally changed in players who played Crystals for as little as six hours. If players can learn to better read and understand the emotional states of others, why not use play in the classroom to encourage improved collaboration and problem solving?

KNOWING TOGETHER MEANS GROWING TOGETHER: DEEPENING CONNECTIONS THROUGH COLLABORATIVE PLAY

Collaborations allow us to grow to our greatest potential as humans. An idea grows wings and flies when multiple people and their ideas are joined. Playful experiences maximize the way in which learners support one another during play. In the ivory towers of higher education, a literature review means reading the theories of all those scholars who've come before you and synthesizing the reading to determine how you can contribute to the research. But it is in regular debate with colleagues that perspectives are shared, context is considered, and new ways of asking questions for future research are revealed.

The way we learn through play is dynamic and dependent on our goals. There is luck involved in game play, much like the luck involved in life. Some folks have affordances that others do not. In play, we can learn with one another in a way that doesn't pit us against one another in a high-stakes way, which may help dismantle some of the many inequities in education. Not every school is laden with devices, nor are the devices we have all used in the best possible way, but creating playful ways to engage with learners lowers the stakes of our interactions and invites different perspectives.

One of my favorite games is a simple card game called Bohnanza, in which each player has their own "field" where they plant and grow different types of beans. The goal is to harvest the highest yield of beans by using strategies that include trading and collaborating with other players. There are limited fields of play, and you can only plant one type of bean in each field, making each valuable territory. A savvy player learns to negotiate with others and makes use of the finite space and resources.

Students delight in the joy of play. The game Bohnanza is both hilarious (stink bean) and laden with learning (strategy, numeracy, probability). This is a game ripe for conversations about simple calculations (multiplication), and it broaches such subjects as scarcity, supply and demand, and even equity and access. And with a few packs of index cards, students can recreate the game with a whole new theme that includes concepts, assets, or themes that are most relevant to what they are learning.

Collaboration through play is another way that connections are deepened and learners connect on meaningful levels. So why not recreate Bohnanza, or a favorite game of your learners, in your own classroom? For instance, taking Bohnanza as a model, students can identify locally grown resources and show others what is unique about their community while also creating a game they can play with their peers and even show off to their siblings.

The corporate world has proprietary tools that encourage people across departments to regularly discuss and check in both formally and informally on their work. Slack channels within a single organization can focus on projects, departments, and even binge-worthy Netflix shows. From commiseration to information sharing to calibration, these check-ins improve the outcomes of our work and give us a sense of belonging.

In the classroom, working with a peer to solve a complicated problem may be called group work in certain instances. But in other instances, it's called cheating and is sanctioned with a note home, a failing grade, or suspension. Real or virtual water-cooler spaces where folks informally discuss their work is where innovative ideas are hatched and optimal solutions are discovered. As adults we acknowledge that solving problems together is key to improving our solutions. Why, then, do we discourage our children from learning collaboratively and growing together each day in the classroom?

From ME to WE through Play

In the famous Bobo doll study by Bandura, people were split into three groups and placed into three separate "waiting rooms," all with the same materials and toys, and told to await the study.[41] Two experimental groups saw a model engaging with the Bobo doll either aggressively (experimental group one) or passively (experimental group two). The control group had no model of any sort.

Results of the study showed that those who observed an aggressive model punching the Bobo doll were more likely to repeat those behaviors, whereas those who were in the nonaggressive control groups did not behave aggressively. While this study has been widely criticized, Bandura's work set the stage for social learning theory and was the impetus for studying group behavior in novel contexts and with different variables.[42,43] It also demonstrates the importance of focusing on and facilitating strong social interactions in classrooms, living rooms, and even boardrooms.

Practicing a little at a time over a long period of time (distributed practice) is a powerful tool for your cognitive toolbox, but it is compounded by the ability to learn with others and applying that knowledge together. Taken together with social learning theory, distributed practice research suggests that facilitating intentional collaborative learning over time may help foster collaboration and even empathy in our classrooms. The way in which we move from *me* to *we* in our professional lives is also relevant in our learning lives. We thrive when everyone knows where they stand and feels like they have a part to play. Driven by interest and fueled by opportunity, our passions can turn into areas of expertise through the sanctionless engagement in collaborative play, where learning together is the reward and improvement is sought with open minds.

MAXIMUM XP

hen OK Go, an American rock band known for elaborate videos, launched their video for the song "This Too Shall Pass," it was an overnight phenomenon. The room-scale Rube Goldberg machine, a contraption that does a simple task in complex and often extraordinary ways, delighted millions across the globe, including my own two children, who watched with glee as the final ball launched a spray of colorful paint at each band member to close out the video. My children were then inspired to integrate a host of new items (is that my toothbrush?) into their own marble runs. So taken was I with this delightful video that I brought it in to show my graduate students. They too found it compelling, and together we discussed how it could be a creative way to teach a variety of concepts, not the least of which are patience and perseverance.

While the video looks seamless, the underlying mechanics of the life-size Rube Goldberg machine in the "This Too Shall Pass" video took six weeks to get just right. The process included engineers, artists, and many other creative types working hard to make certain the contraption was ready for prime time. In fact, according to OK Go's Tim Nordwind, "We've found that most of our ideas, at minimum, take a week and often times months of rehearsal before we feel like we've got something good."[44]

In New Jersey, eighth-grade students in Steve Isaacs's game-design class drew inspiration from both the video of this zany Rube Goldberg machine and the behind-the-scenes footage showing the many attempts necessary to make this machine work. Mashing together his students' innate love of *Fortnite* and their in-class inquiry around simple machines, Isaacs invited students to create a Rube Goldberg machine within the *Fortnite* creative mode. What transpired is a lesson in how very often the game *is* the assessment.

While designing their games, students reflected on the many challenges they faced in achieving their goal. Multiple roadblocks arose during the process—from the trajectory of the baller (the game component that served as the marble completing the course), to the type of pressure pads needed to trigger forward motion. Isaacs asked students to reflect on their iterative designs to make visible the depth and breadth of learning. What could have been a drab lesson on inclined planes, wheels, and axles was transformed by Isaacs into a playful approach to solving problems, bringing purpose to learning.

For this project, there was no summative multiple-choice test about which item in the Rube Goldberg machine represented different aspects of simple machines. There was no homework calculating a fictitious trajectory of an item launched from an inclined plane. Instead, students demonstrated their growing knowledge in practice. Through repetition, failure, and feedback, students emerged with a holistic understanding of how simple machines impact our lives and how knowledge of inclined planes, wheels, axles, and the trajectory of objects in different gravitational fields can actually be put to work. It is knowledge acquired, applied, and secured through play; no external tests necessary. The game is the assessment.

IF YOU BUILD IT, THEY WILL COME

While the nation's policy makers busily revise, update, and perpetuate the use of inequitable standardized tests, our children are learning far more important lessons each day, both in and out of class. The standardized tests, which do little more than perpetuate the status quo in education or, worse yet, act as a continued means of social stratification, fail to take into account so much of the rich learning taking place in our classrooms each day. They also miss the potential of such powerful and impactful learning.

Across a century of research-based findings on successful learning strategies, very few findings, if any, have to do with a regular diet of standardized tests. Instead of using asset-based assessments that call out the deep knowledge that is already *there*, we continue to use traditional deficit-based assessments that are singularly focused on what's *missing*. Research in neuroscience provides evidence that to activate our innate neural plasticity, we need to flip how we currently measure learning and invite more reflection, intention, innovation, voice, and creativity into our learning diets. Essentially, what we're missing to truly innovate in education is more low-stakes playful learning and less rote, rigid, and one-size-fits-all testing. Unsurprisingly, more equitably meeting the needs of all learners may also mean each student receives what they need, not simply the same thing as their grade-level peers the next town over.

Current modes of assessing student learning live in the past and don't take into account the dynamic learning that takes place in classrooms, but many educators are harnessing their superpowers to flip the notion of one-size-fits-all assessment. The science of learning shows that assessment within play can show *learning*, provide *practice*, and demonstrate failures safely while supplying *feedback*.

In this chapter, we'll dive into the cognitive science behind successful learning and see how assessment is inherent in playful and experiential learning experiences. Together we'll explore how the best research we have for learning is actually encapsulated in what most folks think of as child's play. Moreover, we'll see concrete ways in which students are problem solvers, creators, and collaborators in their learning through play, and find ways to make that learning truly visible in order to provide feedback for growth and demonstrate to the world just how much knowledge our kids acquire when they play.

LEVELING UP NONLINEARLY

What I've seen firsthand in teaching students and teachers is what you, dear reader, likely already know: to standardize humans is to lose the essence of what makes us unique and beautiful. We don't all learn the same way and on the same day. Why then should we be beholden to the linear metrics of days gone by?

While humans don't learn in a linear way, there are ways to assess learning that are as dynamic and unique as each of us. Experiential play or games are a natural fit for formative feedback to support the ever-growing neural networks that regulate how we feel, act, and exist in the world. Three simple questions are the foundation for any meaningful assessment. These are the questions I've used as a classroom teacher, a university professor, at home with my own kids, and when prompted for feedback by trusted friends and colleagues: *What do you know? How can you show? Where will you grow?*

In the classroom, these three questions were my written mantra on chart paper (remember those prehistoric times?) using my beloved Mr. Sketch markers. When I removed the caps from the markers, my kids instinctively ran over to determine if brown did, in fact, smell like cinnamon and blue like blueberry. The simple act of recollecting which of the smells aligns with each of the markers is itself an assessment, as well as an interesting commentary on our innate curiosity. Observing my students' natural delight inspires me to seek opportunities for more playful, inquiry-driven learning in order to assess what matters most, the growth and interest of each student, and to find those embedded opportunities to support students in moving forward.

These three simple questions have the potential to improve the learning of each student in a way that meets individual needs and individual interests. Moreover, they help us unpack the unique attributes of each learner, along with the opportunities for areas needing strengthening. In the example of the students in Isaacs's class creating a Rube Goldberg machine in *Fortnite* it is evident that play is learning in practice, with the game itself as assessment. The feedback players receive during play impacts how they move forward and when they feel as if they have completed their goals. It also demonstrates that we are really never done learning. Even the great Einstein once believed the universe was static, yet we now know it is constantly expanding. Just as the universe expands, so, too, does our ability to increase and demonstrate our knowledge.

ASSESSMENT WITHIN PLAY: LEARNING, PRACTICE, FAILURE, FEEDBACK

So how do the three questions above work in practice? Playful learning has assessment built in. Just watch as a child asks to borrow crayons from a peer during art class. Asking a peer for the rust-colored crayon demonstrates cognitive and language skills, social skills of collaboration and cooperation, and even fine motor skills. The student's seemingly simple request can also be used to launch into a conversation about the etymology of the word rust when a crayon appears less red than brown, or it can be an invitation to talk about oxidation.

Interdisciplinary approaches to learning in which students engage through play have the power to exponentially increase not just what students know but how they use that information in the world. Play is a naturally low-stakes environment where mistakes aren't seen as failures but instead momentary setbacks from which we can learn. That same rust-colored apple is no longer an apple in your still-life painting but now an old can of oil next to a tractor in a field.

Mistakes become opportunities for improvisation, setting the stage for an entirely new take on learning. For instance, the Rube Goldberg machine you were programming to launch a marble over the top of two dominoes before continuing its journey may fail and instead knock down the two dominoes. Instead of sweating the setback, you marvel at how those two dominoes set off a whole new chain reaction, opening up an invitation to introduce topics beyond simple machines to increase student understanding of physics. Stated simply, the flexibility play requires helps learners become open to reframing setbacks as opportunities to revise plans while continuing the task alongside others.

In Chapter 4, with the conversation between famed gamers Reverse2K and Ninja, we saw an example of play as formative feedback and an opportunity for improvement. In their communication we see how two people living thousands of miles apart shared an experience of failure and used feedback to find a way to move forward. Imagine if we invited reflections on our students' experiences to be the assessment we use at the end of each term. How differently would school feel for our children and how much more empowered might they be to continue to learn and take on new problems in the future if all learning looked like this?

This is the possibility of play.

THE GAME IS THE ASSESSMENT

So how does play help us level up learning? If we agree that the nature of learning is an ongoing application of knowledge across contexts and experiences, then play is a natural fit for measuring what our students know. Moreover, if we agree that through play our students gain a clearer understanding of the world around them, it becomes clear that playful learning is essential for applied learning. What's more, playful learning may be the most authentic canvas to assess learning because play is dynamic and constantly changing, demonstrating what we've learned and how that learning has room to grow.

In fact, the very best assessments may actually have much in common with what we think of when we think of the word *play*. These assessments are for learning, offer time for revisions and reflection, and include opportunities to demonstrate growth before jumping to the next topic.

Formative, ongoing assessment informs the way we teach our kids while they're learning and provides just-in-time information. This information helps fill in any Swiss cheese holes in their understanding before they move on to different concepts. What's more, summative assignments, like designed projects or interactive presentations and games, demonstrate much more than the acquisition of discrete skills but rather how knowledge is relevant and applicable to the world.

In Chapters 1 through 5, we've seen how play is fluid, dynamic, transformative, and often an inclusive effort toward a shared goal. In this way, the very essence of play is naturally aligned to the most powerful research on learning not through single summative tests but through ongoing formative feedback.

If you think the only thing that *test* and *play* have in common is that they are both four-letter words, I hope this chapter will change your perspective. Better yet, perhaps it will inspire you to infuse into your regularly schedule programming more engaging, playful methods of assessing your learners!

How Working Memory Works

In Chapter 1 we talked about the neural networks underlying human thought, where learning becomes permanent through repeated practice. Messages, or synapses, are sent from one neuron to another, and these synapses strengthen when signaled repeatedly over time, becoming part of a larger network. Adding new practices to existing practices through experience strengthens our neural networks, making our learning more robust over time.

The signaling of synapses in our neurons is the physical manifestation of a learning theory about working memory presented in the late

1960s by cognitive scientists Richard Atkinson and Richard Shiffrin.[45] In studying our curious cerebrum, they hypothesized that our short-term memory requires certain interactions for information to be secured for later recall by our long-term memory. Cue the lights—this is what we educators call simply *learning*! And no, as much as you might try to prove otherwise, there is no such thing as multitasking! Humans can focus on only one cognitively demanding task at a time. Don't believe me? Play along and tell me what you think.

You're driving to the grocery store on your typical route. You're rocking to the latest Beyoncé single at the highest volume when a car pulls out in front of you. What do you do? It is most likely that while slamming on the brakes, you simultaneously turn down the volume. Why is this? Because you can focus on only one cognitively demanding task at a time. The path to your destination is well traveled, so originally you were able to focus on the song, but the moment a wrench (or a car) was thrown into your plan, you had to turn down your tunes to attend to a new stimulus in your environment.

This is all fine and good, but what does it have to do with learning? I'm glad you asked! While we can attend to only one cognitively demanding task at a time, even the attention we can grant to that task is limited by our working memory. Switching between tasks to attend to a new stimulus (the ding of your cell phone that prompted you to respond to a text just now) is not multitasking but serial single tasking. In fact, ample research suggests that serial task switching does a real number on our ability to complete tasks effectively and without error.[46]

Early research in cognition found human working memory capacity is limited to approximately seven (plus or minus two) chunks of information at one time.[47] Legend tells us that this magical number is the reason for the seven digits in Alexander Graham Bell's first telephone numbers. Similarly to the way neuro-cognitive research is providing concrete evidence of what was once abstract, so, too, are new findings providing more concrete evidence of working memory.

What's fascinating is that this magical number of seven (plus or minus two) has persisted for decades! This finding has not decayed as a result of technology use, nor has it changed in tandem with the Flynn effect, which proposes that each generation increases their IQ by approximately three points, perhaps because we're teaching kids to the IQ test.

The net is this: working memory has remained consistent for at least the past seventy years regardless of technology and innovation.[48] So, the question remains: how can we best use our limited cognitive capacity to support learning? The answer includes applied and multimodal practice over time, which sounds an awful lot like play.

Up Your Game: Repetition, Rehearsal, and Timing

Successfully securing knowledge by moving it from working to long-term memory requires repetition, rehearsal, and timing. Returning to the mighty neuron, we see how practice makes knowledge more permanent. Repetition during practice creates a special insulation between connected neurons called myelination.[49] The stronger the myelination, the faster information can be shared. If you'll recall from Chapter 1, the neurons that are connected get stronger, while those that are not regularly used are pruned to make room for new connections and new learning.

More exciting than the knowledge that repetition increases myelination is the fact that neural plasticity extends into adulthood. This means that both children and adults may benefit from practice-induced myelination and the neural plasticity it brings.[50] The rehearsal, associations, and timing of play are powerful opportunities to assess learning and enhance understanding.

While practice makes learning more permanent through myelination, some types of practice are more effective than others. These include distributed, interleaved, and multimodal practice. Each type of practice is enhanced through play, and each can be assessed formatively throughout the school day and year to support ongoing learning and demonstrate the power of experiential play.

Assessment is embedded within the process of play. In fact, play is an organic way to enhance how humans learn. The rehearsal of knowledge associated with multiple representations of information that is practiced over time is embedded in the very nature of play. And this practice is really an ongoing formative and perhaps summative assessment of how acquired knowledge is actually applied in practice. Practicing memorizing one thing does not mean memorizing another will be easier, but the skills you learn in practicing will help you learn in the future.[51]

REPETITION: PRACTICE MAKES PERMANENT

The current regime of standardization through summative tests is not only the opposite of what helps students learn, but it falsely perpetuates a misconception about perfection. Sure, if you practice repeatedly filling in those bubbles, you will master the art of bubbling! But what happens once we realize that artificial intelligence (AI) can more readily respond to multiple-choice questions than a human child? Or when we realize that we've created AI that can generate a more convincing argument in a five-paragraph essay than that same student?

Learning science shows the limits of human capacity next to the possibilities of technology. The implications are not sinister but rather point to opportunities to infuse more experiential and playful learning experiences into the classroom, harnessing the uniquely human abilities of our students and ourselves.

This is not a dystopian future but our current reality. Our innately human abilities, which can be elevated through playful learning, are precisely what we need in a shifting economy. Standardized tests no longer cut it when it comes to identifying what students know and supporting our learners as they apply that knowledge in the world around them. In an evolving economy in which technology is augmenting our ability to learn, connect, and grow each day, it is increasingly clear that human capacity is distinct from machines.

So how then does the mantra of "practice makes permanent" impact learning through play and help us level up the sorts of assessments we use each day? Simple: invite students to elaborate on their play using questions such as: When did you play that last? How has your strategy changed? Why did you change your approach? What about your new strategy seems to be working? How will you know if this new approach is successful? When will you know that you've improved? In this way, your students are the teachers, and the assessment is the play. By asking your learners to reflect on their process, you help them show you just how much they're learning through play each day.

In Level Up 16 you'll find additional questions that help reflect a *student's* approach to learning and growing during play. Asking your kids about the process of play helps them become more reflective thinkers, growing their self-regulated learning skills and enhancing their meta-cognition. In addition, student responses demonstrate how they prefer to receive feedback, so they can continue to grow and create a concrete way to identify with whom they learn during play.

LEVEL UP 16
DEEPENING CONNECTIONS THROUGH COLLABORATIVE PLAY

Questions to ask your learners about their experiences during play
During play. . .
- How are you learning?
- When do you apply learning through practice?
- Where do you receive feedback?
- How do you use feedback to move forward, especially after a setback?
- When do you know that you've mastered learning?

Rehearsal: Repetition over Time as Distributed Practice

In Chapter 5 we saw how distributed practice is inherent in play. We identified distributed practice as an approach that presents smaller chunks of information over longer periods of time with the goal of increasing retention.[52] Time and again researchers find that the distributed presentation, also called *spaced practice*, is a profound practice for teaching and learning.[53]

This approach is in stark contrast to traditional sit-and-get instructional periods followed by time to apply knowledge to practice. Cramming is the antithesis of distributed practice. And while cramming all that good learning into a single all-nighter in college may have helped your recall on the next day's test, it is not an effective way of retaining that information over time. This is not just anecdotal. Empirically based research and experimental studies have found again and again that providing shorter periods of practice over longer periods of time improves learning.[54,55,56,57]

Not only is distributed practice an essential component of long-term learning, the interleaving of concepts during learning shows how it may be applied in different contexts.[58] Interleaved practice is the practice of sharing different concepts or ideas together in a single session. This approach to teaching is a key factor in ensuring we know not only what we're learning but also how it applies to other areas of our lives.

The impact of interleaved practice is based in research and demonstrated time and again in educational settings. A recent study found that introducing students to different artists sequentially increased the ability of learners to distinguish between those artists. In another recent study, two groups of middle-school students learned multiple problem-solving strategies in their math class. The first group learned strategies in blocks while the second learned strategies interleaved. Not only did the students in the interleaved practice group retain the knowledge at a higher rate than those in the blocked group, but those students retained the information for a longer period of time, as evidenced by their recall on a test more than a month later.[59]

In many classrooms, a single concept or problem-solving style is taught in isolation until it is mastered. Even when using distributed practice, or short bursts of information over a long period of time, most instruction focuses on a single concept or approach. For instance, in an art history class, six artists from the Realism genre may be introduced one at a time.

In contrast to teaching a simple approach to solving problems, the interleaved-practice approach asks that multiple approaches be considered in sequence. In the above art history example, this means considering Gustave Courbet *alongside* Rosa Bonheur to appreciate how Courbet erased the imperfections of his subjects as a political statement, as compared to Bonheur's Realist approach to capturing the countryside. Enhancing this approach by introducing the genre of Impressionist art contrasts the free-flowing movement embraced by Monet and Renoir against the more precise and realistic brush strokes of Realists such as Courbet and Bonheur. Interleaved practice not only among artists from the same genre but also across genres helps students discern and remember subtle differences among these otherwise kindred artists. The method of interleaved practice to improve learning is founded in cognitive science, in contrast with traditional instruction, which results in a siloed classroom.

So if the use of interleaved concepts is a key feature of successful learning science, how is this practice observed in play? In Mr. Isaacs's class, while students were creating their Rube Goldberg machines, they had to apply basic knowledge of inclined planes and understanding of the unique gravity within the game, toggle among the multiple sizes and pieces of building materials, and build different types of structures that would both contain and propel their falling objects! No matter the type, all play requires the players to hold multiple ideas simultaneously and learn to attend to different ideas at different times if they are to fully engage in the play. Players must be strategic in the way they approach play, engage with others, and plan, monitor, and assess their own methods. This is yet another reason why cognitive science supports not just learning through play but also using play as the assessment to see where students are at in their learning journey.

SETBACKS AS SUCCESS: FAILURE AS FEEDBACK

Using play to teach and apply content not only flips the script from traditional models of learning but also sends a powerful message that the only time we truly fail is if we don't see our struggles as feedback to fuel us in moving forward. Making mistakes is good for you, as long as you learn what was wrong soon thereafter. Over the past few decades, researchers have looked deeper into the impact of feedback. An interesting shift has been to look at feedback more as fuel for growth after summative assessments and less about traditional, sanction-based approaches. In one study, researchers found that providing feedback to students after a test significantly increased the length of time that the student would recall the information, as demonstrated in a later test.[60] When the correct response is accurately mapped to memory, future recall produces the correct response.

But not all feedback is received equally. Some research has found that the type of feedback that is most beneficial depends on the amount of information you have about the task at hand. A recent study looked at the role of different types of feedback, including verification (immediate correct or incorrect answer feedback), summative (correct or incorrect answer feedback at the end of the assessment), or no feedback at all. Elementary school students were asked to solve math problems and report how they solved the problem. Then they were either given immediate feedback (verification), or no feedback at all. Feedback was based on the numerical answer and not the process children used to solve the problem.[61]

Interestingly, verification (simple yes or no) feedback was beneficial to students who did not have prior knowledge of a correct problem-solving strategy. Moreover, students who held no prior knowledge of the task and who were given simple verification feedback were significantly more likely to work to solve more questions in a later test and to correctly solve later problems.

What happens, however, when students do have prior knowledge? The same study found that verification feedback is detrimental to students with prior knowledge of problem-solving strategies. Specifically, when students with prior knowledge about problem-solving strategies were given verification feedback, they were more likely to use incorrect strategies to solve problems in the future. Perhaps because learners must consider which feedback to focus on, the validation of yes or no, feedback may actually be cognitively taxing in certain instances.[62]

During play your goal is often to do better than you did the last time. There's a lot of self-assessment embedded in leveling up during game play, and it is enhanced with each additional player. While we all learn by watching and playing with others, our self-assessment is based on our strategy, the strategy of our peers, and our ability to use that knowledge to do better next time. In games there's even a term, *replay value*, that refers to the amount of enjoyment a player receives when playing the game repeatedly. Play, fail, learn something, play again trying a new strategy. The persistence we seek is baked into play.

SETBACKS AS EVOLUTION IN LEARNING

In my book *Designed to Learn*, I share dozens of prompts for reflection that are readily translated into formative assessments. Those that invite students to reflect on their learning through both self- and peer assessment reveal, in students' own words, how much they have learned. Perhaps more importantly, setbacks are seen for what they are: feedback. And feedback fuels future actions, whether in play, school, or life.

Failure as an opportunity to iterate is in our DNA. Let's explore for a moment how games capitalize on this, using the board game Evolution as our example. Evolution powerfully models ways that evolved traits that once helped us might later hinder our growth as species. The game may seem complicated at first, but it soon becomes a rich experience laden with opportunity for students to provide self- and peer feedback.

Evolution is an exercise in holding multiple strategies and alliances in mind at once. Players must compete to maintain their species, first herbivores and later, if they so choose, carnivores. The goal is to acquire the largest clutch of points by not only surviving but thriving. Eating food counts toward your point tally, but so do population and traits of your surviving species at the end of the game.

During each turn important actions must be taken before a species is fed. First, you must decide if you're going to evolve your body size or population to acquire more food. However, there must be food available to consume or else your population dwindles. Evolving your species from herbivore to carnivore seems like a good strategy at first. Then you realize that each of the other players has a protective card, and the only available food source is your own species.

It's a rough lesson to be sure, which is why alliances can be key and strategy is constantly changing. Observing others might teach you that playing a foraging card is a good strategy in some instances, but burrowing is often a better trait if you're certain your species has been fed.

The game of Evolution is a lesson in watching and playing with others to grow your own knowledge and skills. As students reflect during play, their goal is often to improve beyond their personal best and feel the power of growth, achievement, and oftentimes patience to try again differently next time. Student reflections often include strategizing for the future while identifying impactful ways in which they have grown as learners.

As with playful learning, in classrooms where the name of the game is reflection, students are empowered to consider what skills and wills are more relevant to their learning. Self-reflective feedback includes what information might be helpful for next time and what their peers have done that might be worth trying in the future. Each of these aspects is critical for growth!

Although self-feedback is very valuable in helping students demonstrate what content they've learned, as well as what content they are still hoping to acquire, peer feedback is uniquely impactful because it allows a student to see themselves through the eyes of someone considered to be more low-stakes than their teacher.[63] Additionally, research shows that learning how to provide specific types of feedback to peers not only solidifies the learners' own skills and knowledge but also enriches their relationships.[64] Level Up 17 provides some useful prompts for students to informally share feedback with their peers or to reflect on their own play by questioning with curiosity and growing together with others.

LEVEL UP 17
SELF AND PEER-REFLECTION AS CRITICAL FEEDBACK FOR GROWTH

While we were playing....
- I didn't understand when/why you ____.
- I wish I had thought to try ____.
- I was really impressed when you ____.
- I wondered what would have happened if ____.
- It was so interesting to see ____.

LEVELING THE PLAYING FIELD

Teachers go through thousands of hours in training programs and learn to assess and support learners in ways that are as unique as each student, but we are then forced to place all of our emphasis of growth on a standardized assessment.

Why do we discount all the valuable feedback and the myriad assessments that teachers give throughout the year in favor of this false panacea of a single summative assessment? Do we really believe that a single score on a single test given on a single day is exemplary of each child's greatest potential? Both you and I know that the answer is a resounding NO!

As educators we have the unique ability to provide feedback that fuels growth, yet so often we're rendered administrators of someone else's canned assessments. Why? Using our own methods of assessment, the feedback we provide solidifies what our students know, helps us see how we can help them grow, and leads to a culture of increased collaboration in the classroom.

So, here's your call to action: when faced with standardized tests that give us a single score for each unique child that is meant to rank and sort individuals into boxes, let's stand up and share the flexible and dynamic assessment we have developed for our learners from their daily classroom experiences. Instead of emphasizing sit-and-get methods to train for multiple-choice questions or the forced and phony essays of standardized assessment, let's rise up and show the growth our children make when we relinquish control, invite purpose and excitement, and learn through playful and rich experiences together.

ALL THE WORLD'S
A SANDBOX:
GROWING UP TO PLAY

I f you've ever wondered why there are only two cable companies to
choose from but seemingly endless pizza places in your town, you are
not alone. To fully understand the relationship between marginal revenue curves and the barriers to market entry as driving factors behind
the zillion pizza joints and two cable companies requires more than one
course in economics. And if you're anything like me, listening to one
lecture on economics is enough to put you off the subject for eternity. So
how are we to understand such a vexing issue?

In our current day, we accept that monopolies don't really serve
consumers well, but that wasn't always the case. In the early 1900s, the
monopolies of Andrew Carnegie and John D. Rockefeller were seen as
beneficial to the consumer. Enter Lizzie Magie, who was born in 1866
in a small town in the Midwest to newspaperman and abolitionist James
Magie and who strongly disagreed with this sentiment.

James Magie gifted Lizzie with the book *Progress and Poverty* around the time of the book's publication in 1879. It was her experience reading this book, along with her exposure to politics and economics as part of a very forward-thinking family, that ultimately drove Lizzie to create the Landlord's Game, or as we now know it, Monopoly. Lizzie's original version of Monopoly was based on the ideas in the book and was essentially created as a tool for teaching, of all things! What's more, included with the game were two sets of rules corresponding to two distinct systems of taxation that could be modeled by game play: monopolist and anti-monopolist.[65]

In the surviving version, only the monopolist rules remain, where a single player might dominate the entire game board. However, Lizzie's anti-monopolist rules introduce a new mechanic in which all players benefit equally when collaborating. Designed as a teaching tool, the goal of the two sets of rules was to reinforce Lizzie's perspective that society as a whole benefits from people working together.

Current research shows that parents continuously explain more complex scientific thinking to their boy children than their girl children.[66] Yet here was Lizzie Magie in the nineteenth century creating a game as a powerful tool to teach complex concepts in economics to everyone. These are concepts that some of us may have failed in undergrad! What Magie offered instead of a lecturing professor was a simple collaborative experience in which you learn by playing. Just as the game is the assessment, the play is the learning.

The duality of Lizzie's two sets of rules can be mapped onto the duality of ways cognitive scientists posit the practice of learning through play. The *how* of learning through play has a duality in terms of place and practice, whereas the *when* of playful learning holds a duality of both developmental appropriateness and proximity to application. Lastly, the *who* in play includes a duality of both roles played and representation and may be a model for how we hope our learners will engage with the world around them today and in the future.

Taken together, the how, when, and who of play encourage us to see the world as a potential sandbox for learning content that is complex and sometimes tedious. While the world as a sandbox is ripe for experimentation, it is also embedded with innate or systemic limitations that impact how, when, and who gets to play and what type of playful and more experiential learning they are afforded.

How Situated Cognition Adds Place to Practice

Educational research has seen a resurgence in studies on experiential learning, or learning by doing, but this method of education actually long predates our current model of public education.[67] Before universal compulsory public education, children learned at the feet of the blacksmith or cobbler. Adults knew that for their children to take on roles in the future, it was essential that they observed and practiced those roles in the places and spaces where they would one day work. Moreover, there was no suggestion that "this child is an auditory learner so we will let them listen to a story of how we will fix a hammer." Instead, children learned to take on that role using the methods that were most appropriate and useful for acquiring that specific knowledge. Often this included many different approaches to learning.

What we have known for ages is that learning is social and requires practice, or play. Play has the potential to tap into the best of situated cognition. While students may not be able to leave the country or even the classroom, they can still try on different roles, and in trying on these new roles, they begin to take different perspectives.

In our current system of compulsory universal public education, this model is often posited as situated cognition. Research has acknowledged that constructing knowledge within the environment where that knowledge will be used is key.[68] With research showing the importance of applied practice, which feels an awful lot like role play, one has to wonder why this type of learning is still not regular practice in classrooms nationwide.

Of course, co-constructing knowledge by active participation is quite difficult with dozens of children learning simultaneously, which is the nature of our current model of compulsory public education. Yet this is exactly the type of experience that builds knowledge through practice. Moreover, the applied fields themselves are often overlooked, ironically, considering the rise in maker spaces, where tinkering and playing is valued, if also labeled STEM. The same actions that years before may have been labeled vocational are now the latest trend, if also given labels such as "robotics." Entrenched within these labels are systemic inequities that often relegate certain learners into one category and others into a completely different learning track. These understandings can be made clear through intentional play.

While playing Monopoly, it may dawn on one player that once a single player owns the majority of the real estate, it's quite difficult for other players to catch up. Although this is not a true experiment in land ownership, it is a simulation that makes the abstract concrete. Play is a natural way to gain deeper insights into important concepts and take on perspectives that may otherwise seem foreign. Moreover, in play the concepts that are too difficult to simply read about become crystalized through experience.

Lizzie Magie's earliest version of Monopoly invites players to participate in learning through play based on two different sets of rules. Through repeated game play, it becomes clear how in one instance (e.g., landlord's game) the early real estate investors (landlords) quickly accrue significant profits difficult to broach by most other players, whereas in the other version of game play (e.g., single tax) the impact of turning private spaces, such as game reserves, into public goods, such as colleges, is quickly seen.

Play to Practice in the Modern Day

Modern-day equivalents for leveraging playful learning to ignite situated cognition are abundant. Both analog and digital playful experiences are available to give learners an inside view of concepts and issues of great importance. For instance, while a class trip to the nation's capital provides an impactful opportunity to learn about the way our government enacts legislation, that kind of trip is out of reach for many of our schools and students. However, by playing LawCraft by iCivics, students can take on the role of legislators enacting laws.

In LawCraft, each student plays as a member of Congress, taking an issue of importance from their constituents and working to move their bill successfully through the legislative process. To win the game, a player must not only pass a bill, but also show that they understand an issue of importance to their community. The situated cognition in which you apply learning in practice is enhanced when the lens of perspective adds the potential for a player to develop a sense of empathy for another, as when a player takes on a community issue.

When content is meaningfully infused into play, learning becomes more enjoyable. And while our students may not be able to board a mission to Mars just yet, they can certainly role play as mission control specialists, members of Congress, or doctors in an emergency room. Certainly, students are not able to take on surgery after a laugh-filled game of Operation, but this seemingly silly game does allow them to hone their hand-eye coordination and fine motor skills, and with a few hacks to put the organs in the correct locations, students can understand just how complex it is to reach a spleen in its location beneath the ribs.

In fact, education is not the only industry harnessing situated cognition as a powerful mechanism for learning by doing. Across industries, people across the life span and experience levels are learning through simulations. The government has used virtual simulations to practice for work on a military base for decades. More recently, virtual reality has been used to help prepare for work in emergency rooms. Human resources departments are integrating similar experiential or playful learning exercises into trainings to improve work, from stockrooms to boardrooms and everyplace in between. This move to infuse playful and experiential learning is evidence that the space *where* you play is often as important as *how* you play.

In Level Up 18, we see how to apply play to practice in the classroom in a way that highlights the skills and wills students acquire during learning. We can upgrade learning through play the same way items and characters are improved through upgrades in game play. More importantly, the learning that happens naturally through play provides an opening to talk about roles in our current society. In discussing these roles, we can begin to take the perspective of others whose experiences and understanding vary from our own and begin to see how different areas of expertise have their own languages (e.g., the language of music)!

LEVEL UP 18
APPLYING PLAY TO PRACTICE IN THE MODERN DAY

How can educators use play to enhance situated cognition for ALL students? What are the tools?	• Analog (e.g., card games) • Digital (e.g., computer, tablet, laptop) • Immersive (e.g., virtual reality, augmented reality)
What skills are embedded within the content students can learn through play?	Example: The card game Forbidden Island teaches about the roles of a pilot, engineer, and explorer, which can map on to learning in social studies (cardinal direction, navigation, topography), science (collecting and analyzing data, design and test solutions), and language arts (communicating for clarity).

WHEN YOU DON'T USE IT, YOU MAY LOSE IT

The *how* of learning requires enacting novel roles during play, which provides the opportunity to co-construct meaning, learn by doing, and more importantly practice perspective taking as we experience life as an "other." The *when* of play extends to the time and place in which we're learning. The duality of *when* references the developmental appropriateness of playful learning experiences and the proximity to application, meaning that the when of play not only refers to the age of the player but also the timing of when information is shared, so that it comes at just the right time to be readily applied.

In Level Up 19 we harness the power of *when* in play, specifically examining how playful learning provides the opportunity to provide just-in-time feedback, and how timing of play is naturally complementary to the way in which learners grow. By considering the possibilities of when to infuse play into learning, along with anticipating the potential outcomes of that play, you are setting your learners up for timely and fruitful learning.

LEVEL UP 19 QUESTIONS THAT HARNESS THE POWER OF WHEN IN PLAY	
When can play help enhance and support development?	• What type of play is developmentally appropriate for the students you're working with? • When can this type of play be incorporated in the classroom? • How can play be scaffolded to become increasingly complex through development?
How does play provide just-in-time opportunities for feedback?	• Where are there just-in-time opportunities to use play to reinforce a concept with intention AND flexibility? • How does just-in-time feedback support learning and growth? • When will you assess the outcomes of the playful learning in your classroom and how will you share student growth with students and their caregivers?

Playful learning is much like guided inquiry.[69] In the guided inquiry model, students have access to relevant information and intentionally placed scaffolds as they approach learning. As in the game of Clue, the information is all there, and it is up to you to decipher whodunnit! Unlike other models, such as discovery learning or open inquiry, where open exploration is cognitively taxing and detracts from the goal, play is like guided inquiry. There is less of a chance that a student will stumble upon a resource that is irrelevant, inappropriate, or downright incorrect.

Play enhances the self-determination of learners in typical guided inquiry. Students must work with one another and in doing so, are able to demonstrate their competence, autonomy, and relatedness within agreed-upon parameters. Because it is guided, play address the duality of *when*, as it can be both developmentally appropriate and provide just-in-time information for students to use; in using that information, they will retain it much longer.

In commercially available games, the parameters of play might include a game board, the rules, a sequence of actions you can take, as well as the ultimate goal of the game. In student-created games, the guided parameters of rules, actions, and goals are co-created. For instance, in the game Evolution, the goal is to evolve creatures that can feed on the available food and be the player with the largest population, most traits, and the largest storage of food at the end of the game.

When I first began playing the game Evolution with my fourth- and sixth-grade students, their immediate desire was to evolve a carnivore that could hunt all our creatures! Slowly, over the first two game plays, they started to grasp the advantage of certain traits over others and began applying their understanding of why a burrowing creature has an advantage over one with a long neck—just in time to face a predator.

Most games have the potential to grow alongside a child's growing knowledge, and the fun often becomes adding rules to make play more complex. The game Anomia can be as simple or complex as the players around the table, meeting the needs and engaging learners on multiple levels. Players take turns flipping over a card from the draw deck and placing it in front of them until a player draws a card that has a symbol matching the symbol on another player's card. Then the first of those two players to shout out an example of the item listed on the other player's card wins both cards. As play progresses, a simple and straightforward game mechanic gets increasingly complex and often faster.

In neither Evolution nor Anomia are players actually practicing measuring liquids, drafting a bill to Congress, or designing an earthquake-proof home. But in each instance, simply playing leads to learning that can be scaled to meet the needs of the learner, who then gets feedback just in time to use their new knowledge to be even more successful in the future. There is no reason why Anomia cannot be hacked to include theories of relativity, literary tropes, or significant historical events.

Games like Monopoly have complicated strategies that little ones can't necessarily absorb as readily as older learners, but even the youngest players can roll the dice and count the squares, then watch in delight as the little dog token moves around the board. Older players can be the banker, making change for players who land on an unclaimed piece of real estate. These are precisely the interdisciplinary and multi-age learning environments that preceded our more industrial models of education. When learners of different ages, interests, and backgrounds are grouped together, students learn and grow with and from one another.

However, that doesn't mean students in traditional classroom settings, where only students of the same age play together, can't modify games to meet their specific needs and areas of interest. Perhaps instead of playing Monopoly with the purpose of acquiring real estate and generating revenue, your middle-school students could use the same game board to focus on addressing sustainable development goals. Players may instead find success in reducing their carbon footprint, decreasing the economic impact of moving toward renewable energy sources, and addressing the ecological impacts of deforestation on global communities. The goal of the game and the opportunities to extend the learning to the wider world is predicated solely on the interest of the student.

The information-processing model of knowledge acquisition shows that if we receive information when we need it, we are most likely to retain it in long-term memory for future retrieval. In play as in life, we seek out information we need at the moment we need it. In fact, researchers have found that when students explore content before explicit instruction, they often enjoy superior learning outcomes.[70] Presenting a puzzle or an intriguing problem ahead of potential solutions may help prime students for learning when a specific concept is later taught.

Play also provides a sense of guided inquiry, not an open free-for-all but a deliberate pathway toward a specific outcome. A significant benefit of guided inquiry through play is that students are not cognitively taxed with the additional burden of seeking out accurate information while simultaneously solving a problem. This intuitive approach to learning just in time also allows us to recall information when it is needed again later.

The downside to guided inquiry through play is that students are not explicitly taught to distinguish fact from fiction. However, the upside is that media literacy itself can be an experience or game to play. Over time the skills of media literacy and identifying the best potential sources for an argument are honed, but in the near term students have the information they need at their fingertips and can focus on using that knowledge to solve problems.

WHOSE ROLES, WHOSE RULES: REPRESENTATION EMBEDDED IN LEARNING THROUGH PLAY

We've all had the experience of hearing once about a concept and then suddenly seeming to find it all around us! There's a term for this effect: the *frequency illusion*.[71] This illusion is a cognitive bias that explains why once you've heard the words "cognitive bias" you'll seem to hear them all the time!

It's not necessarily that they are being used more regularly but that once you know what you didn't know before, that knowledge seems to be all around. This important lesson extends to all our work as educators. If we don't know what we don't know, how do we acquire knowledge that is missing today so we have access to that information tomorrow?

The roles of players are as varied as the types of play our students wish to engage in and act as means to support our students in learning new information while seeing things from new perspectives. While everyone has different interests, there is always room to learn and grow together. Play is a natural conduit for exploring novel roles and launching into inquiry about the roles we see around us and the evolving set of rules we humans follow each day.

Anyone who has played Monopoly with multiple children knows that determining who rolls first or who plays as the coveted kitten token is itself an opportunity for situated cognition as negotiator in a war zone. All kidding aside, the roles our children take on through play provide an opportunity to put their learning to practice, to consider how it feels to play as an "other," and to think about the assumptions embedded in our own thinking each day.

While playing Monopoly with students, perhaps we should consider the histories of those who have created the games or even the roles embedded in that play. As she researched Lizzie Magie, author Mary Pilon wondered, "How many other buried histories are still out there—stories belonging to other lost 'Lizzie Magies' who quietly chip away at creating pieces of the world, their contributions so seamless that few of us ever stop to think about the person or people behind the idea?"

In the course of playing Monopoly, players can experience many roles. They experience the role of a landlord earning rent when others land on their property, but they also learn the role of the tenant, when an unlucky roll lands them on Park Place, an expensive property made even more so by the presence of multiple hotels. Worse yet, they may take on the perspective of the individual stuck in jail, unable to pay the fine for release and therefore missing valuable turns to emerge from their unlucky lot. This can be a profound moment of understanding and an opportunity for difficult discussions.

In her work researching Lizzie Magie's creation of Monopoly, Pilon noted, "On some level, Lizzie understood that the game provided a context—it was just a game, after all—in which players could lash out at friends and family in a way that they often couldn't in daily life. She understood the power of drama and the potency of assuming roles outside of one's everyday identity." As we've seen from the research, we learn and grow through play. What Pilon identifies here is that play can be an important space where together we can struggle through obstacles and emerge with a new understanding. Moreover, we can use play to explore our very identities in ways that are safe and flexible but also meaningful and applied.

In this way, the play itself becomes an exploration of both who the game was designed *for* as well as who it was *not* designed for. For instance, how is the play a representation of a specific individual's perspective and their understanding of the world around them? What assumptions are embedded in a player's decision to take the role of explorer or novelist, chemist or jockey? These questions demand that we consider the prior knowledge needed to take on certain roles in the first place, the latent ableism in enacting these activities, the access one has to information, and the affordances of each role.

In Level Up 20, we explore the possible roles, representations, and assumptions embedded in play. In exploring representation, or what roles are available, we're also inherently looking at what roles and what representations are missing from play. It is then that we can start to unpack our latent biases in the assumptions we make through play and apply those hard truths to the world around us.

LEVEL UP 20 ROLES, REPRESENTATION, AND ASSUMPTIONS IN PLAY	
Roles	• What roles are possible in this game? • Who typically holds these roles? Who wants to hold these roles but has yet to be included? Why?
Representation	• What roles are represented and what are some roles that are missing? Why are those roles not seen here? Do these omissions tell us anything about those who have a voice and those who do not?
Assumptions	• What assumptions are embedded within each role? Prior knowledge, ability, interest, access, affordance?

Cognitive biases like the frequency illusion can actually be helpful in priming our learners to be aware of assumptions in the world around them during play. For instance, how many women are represented in play? What roles do those women hold? Who has the power during play, and how is that power distributed?

Each question tests an assumption embedded in play, but it does more than that. It allows us to have more meaningful conversations with our students, who are flexibly adopting new roles through play. If we can prime students to notice assumptions in play, perhaps we, too, will be primed to grow through identifying assumptions and seeking ways to be better.

Our role as educators is sometimes to listen, to ask questions, and to quietly observe. But other times our role is active and assertive as we usher students out of their shells and into new ways of thinking and acting in the world. By modeling our own continued growth, moving forward despite making mistakes, and asking questions for clarity to remove any latent bias, we are actively driving toward a more robust nature of learning.

MORE THAN A SCORE

Kennedy Gardens Elementary School is one of six elementary schools serving children in Calexico, California. The city straddles the Mexico–United States border and is one of six cities that together make up the Imperial Valley region. Agriculture accounts for roughly 70 percent of all jobs across the Imperial Valley, which students at Kennedy are keenly aware of.

When teacher Jesus Huerta began his Bloxels game project, a simple building tool in which students create their own video games, students wondered why programming was important in a city known for its agriculture. What they would soon discover is that the creation of games is rich with learning opportunities that can be applied to many different industries, from design and film to business and agriculture.

Huerta is inspired by flexible technologies that his students can use as tools to playfully create their own experiences. This inspiration birthed the project, in which students design their own game by first developing a narrative for their story. "In order to have an awesome game, you have to have a great story," explains Huerta.

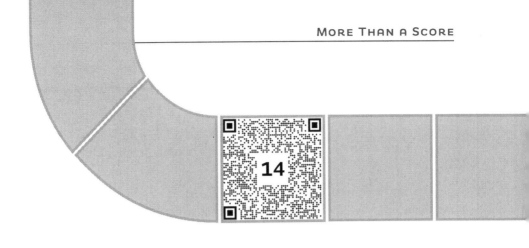

As a fellow child of the '80s, I was impressed with Huerta's use of Perler pegboards for students to piece together eight-bit versions of their main character. Using the Bloxels app, Huerta's invites student to bring their games to life beginning with a narrative, rich character development, and then a clear storyboard. This work results in games that are regularly a resounding success, as evidenced by the Fall Games Festival Huerta hosts at his school. Huerta plastered the eight-bit Perler images, storyboards, and even narrative essays all over the room, while laptops were opened at each desk, providing students with a gallery to play with all the games. The entire school community joined in the celebration of the games, and as students played games created by their peers, they learned about the diverse interests of their friends and saw all of the creative work that goes into creating the games they love to play.

"You want to work in farming one day, right?" Mr. Huerta asked his students. "Knowing how to code through robotics will help you program your tractors! And if you love to draw, did you know that you can be a designer that creates storyboards for games or movies?" The work of Huerta and his students is the crowning achievement of our humanity: the ability to create something beautifully unique.

Why then would we want to standardize these incredible humans or force worksheets upon them when learning coordinates on a plane is so much richer, estimating numbers in a calculation so much more meaningful, and problem solving toward a creative solution so much more impactful when done through play?

In Play, the Process Is the Product

In play, a score is never set in stone, and the goal is often to be better than you were the last time. Isn't this also how school should be? Mr. Huerta's class shows that it's not about the game but rather the process of exploration and discovery that makes playful learning powerful. Frankly, the ability to pivot and try something new without fear of retribution is what makes play feel like magic. As students learn new skills, they adapt their understanding to revise and improve the games they create. All the while, children are connecting with one another and growing together. Instead of a one-size-fits-most approach, play affords players the opportunity to grow alongside more knowledgeable others in some instances, or as the more knowledgeable player at other times. Play values our unique contributions and invites growth in a more equitable way, whereby players get what they need to succeed at the right time and in the way that works best for them.

During play, we are more at ease. Our inhibitions are often set aside while we give way to the flow that is exploration and discovery. This is in direct contrast with traditional modes of learning that are predicated on single opportunities to know the right answer and move along. In fact, the pressure-filled experiences found in many of our classrooms may actually turn off our ability to learn. Compliance-based sanctions and accountability systems put our children and our teachers on high alert. While the steroid hormone cortisol is helpful in regulating inflammation and blood pressure, when it is triggered by stress it significantly reduces our ability to focus on anything other than a perceived danger in the environment around us.

The relationship between the feeling of danger and the ability to grow and discover in a learning environment is well documented in academic research. In fact, there's an entire chapter in the book *Biobehavioral Markers in Risk and Resilience Research* dedicated to environmental and relational impacts on children from early childhood.[72] What has become clear is that the more rigid and inflexible the environment or the relationship, the higher the levels of cortisol.

But it is not just relationships and environments in school that matter. Each of our children come to school with experiences that will impact the way they "are" in the classroom. The well-known research around adverse childhood experiences (ACEs) highlights factors most detrimental to growth and development. It is no surprise that factors outside our children's control, such as an incarcerated family member or a violently treated mother, will significantly impact our kids' ability to function in their classrooms each day.[73] Perhaps most striking about the ACEs research is the long-term impact of these ecological factors. While educators cannot remove the detrimental ecological experiences our children face, research does indicate that creating a climate of care can positively impact learning outcomes.

Free and focused play provides the guided inquiry that supports learning, but it is our feedback and the way we facilitate camaraderie among our learners that creates a positive and open culture of learning. The way we invite students to support one another acknowledges that knowledge is subjective and learning is not a linear pathway for each student. But can the environment change the way our bodies release hormones in a single learning period?

In a fascinating study of the effects of climate on perception and cortisol, undergraduate participants were randomly assigned to one of two groups: ego-involving or task-involving.[74] Participants in the ego group each focused on themselves while the task group focused on learning the task at hand—in this case juggling. Each group had both an instructor and a staged participant (called a confederate) as part of the experiment. The confederate was proficient at juggling but pretended to learn alongside participants to aid the instructor in changing the climate.

Each group was given the goal of learning to juggle to prepare for a championship match between the two teams at the end of the lessons. While the goals and activities that each group was assigned were exactly the same, the feedback participants received while learning was different.

In the ego group, the instructor was putative, punishing mistakes and pitting participants against one another. Additionally, in the ego-involving group the confederate pretended to learn more quickly than his peers. The confederate was also given more praise by the instructor, which perpetuated the climate of competition. Instead of helping to teach others in his group, the confederate relished the praise and carried on improving his own skills.

By contrast, the instructor in the task group spoke to all participants equally and encouraged teamwork. When the confederate in the task-involving group appeared to learn juggling more quickly, that individual was asked to support his peers. The task, of course, was for each individual to learn to juggle in order to make the group better as a whole. Only later would they compete against another group for the championship.

The researchers collected a variety of data points. Oral samples were collected at multiple points to determine changes to the cortisol levels. Participant self-reports about aspects of their internal motivation, perceptions of climate, and cognitive stress were also repeatedly collected.

Not surprisingly, the results of data analysis showed that participants in the ego group had stronger feelings of shame, negative affect, and stress. The participants in the ego group also reported a significantly higher level of social evaluation, harkening back to Bandura's idea of models and how we compare ourselves to others, than those in the task group. What's more, they reported feeling lower levels of control over their learning. And they had increased cortisol levels. By comparison, participants in the task group demonstrated a greater interest in learning the task along with a more pleasurable overall experience and lower levels of cortisol.

These results point to a powerful protective physiological response when individuals are in supportive environments. That the behavior of others may trigger the release of cortisol, potentially impacting your ability to learn, should be all we need to know to put an end to stress-induced learning. Sayonara, high-stakes testing!

If You Build It, They Will Come (Eventually)

When I spoke with Jesus Huerta about his work with students at Kennedy Gardens, he shared that the inspiration behind his gameful project was Caine's Arcade. The 2012 viral phenomenon hit as my own children were starting formal education and I was struggling with how they might fare in a system made to place people in boxes.

The story of Caine's Arcade starts with a precocious nine-year-old boy with an incredibly supportive family. The supportive family piece is key, as Caine is invited to not only set up a cardboard arcade in his father's auto-parts store but also is allowed to keep the arcade games standing for a week. Those of us who've worked in early childhood know how hard it is to ask children to take down their marvelous towers in the block center if only to ensure other kids have time to build their Rube Goldberg machine after lunch.

Using old shipping boxes, Caine created cardboard arcade games complete with tickets after game play, a prize board, and even a "fun pass" that offers five hundred game plays for a mere two dollars. At one point he asks his father for a claw machine to add to his arcade and is met with the question, "Why don't you build it yourself?" Caine quickly gets to work using an S-hook and string, and to everyone's delight is successful in creating his very own claw machine.

The video of Caine building his arcade is at once inspiring and, for those of us working with children, pretty unremarkable. I don't mean to say that children aren't extraordinary. Quite the opposite. When you've worked with kids for years, you know children are innately capable of so much more than we give them credit for. Their latent creativity lies dormant while traditional schooling pushes worksheets and notebooks.

When one customer, Nirvan Mullick, comes in for a door handle for his '96 Corolla, he's instantly taken with the arcade and decides not only to buy a fun pass—"A pass is an awesome deal!"—but also to create a ten-minute video to share Caine's story with the world. And when young Caine is met with disbelief from his friends that he does in fact own an arcade, Nirvan plans a surprise flash mob to surprise him.

It's hard not to well up when you see Caine's father watch as traction for the surprise flash mob grows. Watching this proud father read comment after comment from people across the globe is an exercise in inspiration. Each person shares that they're more disappointed than the next that they can't make it to East L.A. because they live in Tennessee, New York, and EUROPE! *I'm* not crying, *you're* crying! No really, I dare you to watch the video and not cry.

But this is not the point. The point is that without any reason other than that they can, children will always play. When supported by grown-ups, our children's play will proliferate. And when we connect to our innately playful selves, we may also be released from the shackles that hold us back. We are free to ask questions for clarity, to seek solutions without fear of looking foolish, and to begin our work again tomorrow.

RECYCLE THAT CAN AND CREATE PLAYFUL CHANGE

For far too long, a canned curriculum and its aligned worksheets have been the standard for learning and measuring growth in our country. If you've read this far, you're likely on board with tossing that canned curriculum in the recycling bin and working to co-create the meaningful learning possible that arise when we give our kids the room to explore and play.

The climate we create has the power to significantly impact the way our kids learn each day. Research findings like those about cortisol increasing in response to stressful environments are hardly news to most educators. And the idea of differentiated instruction is itself likely an outgrowth of watching our children on the playground. Our kids don't naturally divide themselves based on their reading level when the grown-ups aren't looking, so why are we forcing our kids into specific boxes when in reality they want to explore all of the boxes, pyramids, and balls on the playground?

The study on climate and cortisol was an impactful reminder of the stark difference between classrooms where there's a stoplight behavior chart at the front of the classroom and those where there is flexible seating and a low hum of noise with no obvious front to the classroom. When we overcontrol, we leave less room for creativity and flexibility and, interestingly enough, we end up with significantly lower test scores.[75]

While play is not a magical panacea to cure everything that ails our nation's youths, taking a more playful and process-oriented approach to learning may help assuage student fears of being wrong. Working together as a team, lending support, offering feedback, and focusing on the task and not an innate "ability" that you just can't put your finger on are all beneficial aspects of play. In some games you'll see this in practice. It's called *level scaling*, and it's a way to create equity by making challenges appropriate to the player.

As fluid, flexible, and open to iteration, play sits at the opposite end of our current system of public education that is fixed, rigid, sanction-based, and putative. Yet these essential elements of play that ignite inspiration and a desire to learn are significant to every educator, parent, and child. It is the flexible and multimodal attempts at solving problems through play that drive inquiry and understanding.

But it's not just any kind of trying that results in learning. We all know that the definition of trying the same thing over and over and expecting different results is the definition of insanity. Learning is a result of trying in different ways on different days to make meaning out of something that compels us—an itch we just have to scratch, a problem we just have to solve, or an opportunity we just can't let walk away.

So how can we do this more intentionally? I'm so glad you asked.

Boss-Level Territory: Multiple Entry Points to Play

Offering multiple opportunities for students to play together also ensures our kids grow together. Countless games offer students the opportunity to take on the perspective of others and learn to work together in order to succeed. Many well-known cooperative games make for excellent classroom play. These include Hanabi, in which players work together to create the perfect firework show; Pandemic, in which participants work together to stop a pandemic from spreading across the globe; and Forbidden Planet, the role-playing game described at the beginning of Chapter 3. Each of these low-fi games is infused with just the right excitement to invite repeated play. What's more, each can be hacked to create a novel experience based on the learning happening in your classroom.

Prepare yourself to earn your boss-level badge in Level Up 21. Here you'll find essential questions and suggestions for placing your students at the center of learning in a place they gravitate toward naturally: play! For your last mission you'll become a "boss" by thinking differently about an existing game or playful experience, hacking a favorite playful experience to make it your own, and making the ultimate leap toward creating next level learning through play.

LEVEL UP 21 BOSS LEVEL	
Existing Game	• Remember your favorite games from Level Up 4? What existing games are you seeing differently now from when you started reading? From Tetris to Trivial Pursuit, what ways are these games making learning more purposeful and fun? • What is something this game has taught you that you hadn't realized until right now? Who is one person you could share that realization with and invite to join in you in this game play?
Hack a Game	• Thinking about the games you love from Level Up 4, what playful experience could you recreate with your own spin? What are the mechanics of this game, or the rules for play, that could help teach something in a new way? What would this new game look like? What could you learn from it and how would it work?
Create a New Game	• If you had a magic wand and could create the ultimate game, what would it look like? Who would you invite to join you in co-creating this game? What would this new game teach (content but also ways of being together and collaborating)? • How would this game be more inclusive of others who don't see themselves in current games?

One of my favorite examples of this type of hacking is how university professor Dr. Matt Farber flipped the card game One Night Ultimate Werewolf into a tool to teach about the perspective of characters in *The Crucible*.[76] By inviting students to create the play while also taking the perspective of its characters in, Farber brilliantly inspired not only active engagement in a decades-old piece of literature but cultivated joy in learning. Utter magic!

UNDERSTANDING LIFE THROUGH PLAY

In today's world, technology is an important topic, especially in regard to putting it to good use. In the commercial card game Control-Alt-Hack,

players take of the role of ethical hackers and use networking, hardware, and software knowledge to help accomplish missions.[77] Players demonstrate a significant increase in learning after game play.

Similarly, through the activities and games on Project KidHack, curated by NovaInfosec, students and teachers can learn together about cyber security, hardware, software, and the foundations of coding.

GENERATIVE GAMES: CONTRIBUTING TO THE FUTURE THROUGH GAMES

A number of particularly exciting opportunities for game play exist in the field of life science, including games that allow participants to interact with scientists and potentially impact real-life research. But first let's take a look at a more low-fi game that your students will love. In Cycles, players as young as eight can compete to complete life cycles for one of thirteen different creatures, all while wielding secret powers just like those found in nature. This leads to competitive and hilarious game play that can be completed within a single class period, indoor recess, or rainy afternoon. Moreover, games like Cycles breathe new life into classrooms where the tired texts from years gone by are outdated, confusing, and, frankly, just dull. Instead of another drag-and-drop worksheet, players learn by doing, engaging, and even laughing alongside their peers.

For a more high-tech playful experience that invites active discovery in the world around, you can't beat iNaturalist as a tool for inviting more collaborative and intentional play. Equipped with a smartphone, anyone can be a biologist helping to document invasive plant species taking over a garden or a rare butterfly not typically seen in this hemisphere. At the elementary level, the traditional neighborhood walk at the beginning of the school year becomes a grander adventure with iNaturalist. More advanced learners can help document changes to biodiversity by snapping photos of species. Using the recently added taxon frameworks, student researchers can now work in collaboration with expert scientists across the globe. While still requiring a device, the ability to collaborate with scientists from wherever you're sitting surely is a step toward more equitable access to high-quality learning experiences than ever before.

Over the years, iNaturalist users have documented more than a hundred thousand different species. What's more, citizen scientists have helped identify rare creatures. In 2014, one user uploaded an image of a snail that was later identified as a species described by James Cook's crew in the 1700s yet never before photographed.

On May 1, 2019, iNaturalist launched the Half-Earth Project in honor of American biologist, naturalist, and author Edward O. Wilson. Now people the world over can document and map species in their own environments. On nature walks, during recess, and even on a walk around our school building, we can document the living creatures in our environment in an effort to conserve half of the earth's lands and seas to preserve biodiversity. How cool is that?

Multiple other ways exist for students to become citizen scientists through games. Two particularly noteworthy ones, which are focused on biology, are Eterna and Foldit. Dr. Jennifer Doudna, Professor of Molecular and Cell Biology and Chemistry at UC Berkeley, believes that "there's an interesting interplay between the process of doing science and the way that games work."

This interesting interplay was the impetus for the citizen-science game Eterna, in which players grow their knowledge of RNA to aid

researchers in seeking cures for diseases from malaria to cancer.[78] Within the game is a simulation called OpenCRISPR, through which players learn about the unique role of RNA, unlocking increasingly complex levels as they play. "Science has always been a series of puzzles to solve; that's what makes it fun," says Dr. Doudna.

But Doudna and her faculty at UC Berkeley don't just believe that games can make science fun; they think that all people should be part of a global lab. If we are to solve some of our greatest ailments, they believe we should be doing this together, as a community.

To put their beliefs into practice, Stanford researchers take players' designed solutions out of the game simulation and into the lab. Doudna and her colleagues work to synthesize and test successful designs to see how they work in practice. The feedback from each test is then shared with the players who devised each solution, who are then invited to further innovate upon and revise their solutions.

By inviting in a wide community of players, the researchers hope to design a set of guiding principles for how RNA functions in order to improve the way we edit genes and tackle a host of human diseases. The most exciting aspect of this work is the knowledge that automation does not substitute for human creativity. Only with the broad and diverse perspectives and unique creativity of many players will the most successful patterns emerge. What Eterna has shown us is the power of any person to essentially collaborate with scientists and help solve the puzzles of the deadliest human diseases.

Likewise, the game Foldit, which took the world by storm in 2008 when it was released by researchers at the University of Washington, leverages a global community in an attempt to solve dizzying and dazzling puzzles. Foldit players must determine the structure of proteins, of which there are hundreds of thousands in the human body. Using a simple yet compelling game mechanic, players quickly learn how different proteins behave in completely distinct patterns. Players then became solutionaries working alongside scientists to discover novel models of proteins whose structures could impact the cures we create for cancer, Alzheimer's, and HIV.

With games like Eterna and Foldit, as well as iNaturalist and Cycles, science is no longer a feared subject or a faraway goal but instead an accessible challenge. The potential impact of play could not be made any more real than by watching as students document endangered species or find a protein pattern that aids in the discovery of a much-needed vaccine. Like unlocking a previously unknown level in *Super Mario*, with purposeful practice players unlock new and exciting levels of learning through play.

BUILDING A GLOBAL COMMUNITY

It is easy to be awed by the RNA-replication game Eterna and the protein-folding game Foldit. In each one a seemingly simple and playful experience has drawn in millions of players who together have discovered potential cures for our deadliest diseases. This is powerful stuff, but it does not have to be relegated solely to the science classroom!

Together we've seen the infinite ways we grow through play. Moreover, we've seen how the process of play is as important as the product of our play (that's the winning part). Simultaneously, we see that cognitive and emotional growth are supported through play, bringing a new understanding of how we can support students in taking perspective.

Taken together it becomes clear that the seemingly simple act of play may actually improve our ability to empathize with others. Perhaps we could even use play to create a global community of collaborators, working together to solve the most pressing problems of our future. This is

likely the impetus for John Hunter when he created the World Peace Game in 1978 to simulate the infinite complex scenarios embedded with international peacekeeping.

Using a simple plywood gameboard, the World Peace Game invites students to play on behalf of one of four nation states. They play for different nations but have a single goal: solving all the world's problems without combat. At first glance it appears to be a simple premise, but the plot thickens as the game unfolds.

The layers of game play include both the physical (sea, land, air, outer space!) and the figurative (philosophical, military, and economic differences). What then emerges may be a more concrete understanding of equality. Do we all need the same amount of resources, versus equity, or do we need to distribute those resources so everyone who needs, has?

Play that will take learning to the next level will leverage our unique perspectives as humans alongside our growing technological capacities as creators. In 1978, the World Peace Game was ahead of the game. And while many of the principles remain the same and the concrete representation of assets on a map are essential for understanding, we now have the ability to map on new ways of learning about policy making across the globe.

WHEN OLD'S COOL

Creating playful learning means reframing the goal of a lesson as a chance to play. How can I teach multiplication without using digital or analog flashcards? Simply placing facts on a device is not automatically playful. Before we had fancy technology, the abacus worked quite well for teaching multiplication facts and still provides a solid foundation to extend our innate number sense (we're ALL math people, people!). But it's also a multimodal tool for exploration. What other old school tools can be repurposed for learning?

Inspiration abounds across the globe of educators upcycling materials to create games just like those in Caine's Arcade. Basic elements of gravity, physics, spatial reasoning, and even probability are conversations that can arise while creating an upcycled marble run. Find a new use for paper plates, empty toilet paper rolls, or even pool noodles by creating a marble run, no tech necessary (except to see the ingredients for this recipe for fun and learning).

The brilliant folks of WeAreTeachers have a host of inspiring board game hacks that turn old school toys into new opportunities for engagement. They include a customized game of Guess Who? in which students have to ask questions of one another to guess the dinosaur. Can't you just hear the squeals of laughter as students wonder, "Does it have a brain larger or smaller than a Brazil nut?" (Answer: it's a Stegosaurus!)

Other hacks of old school games completely transform Trivial Pursuit. For instance, a hack by Suzy from Student Savvy has students "battle it out" to collect cards of creatures for each unique biome. This could work for any content area and any age of student if the cards collected are historical figures, categories of elements in the periodic table, or even categories of philosophy.

Still not feeling challenged? Why not activate your students' neural networks and flip prehacked games from teacher to student created?

Students can curate their own knowledge and create their own versions of older games. Breathing new life into Uno, Life, Monopoly, or Go Fish is a chance to step away from the screen, use their hands, and create!

And if you're still feeling adventurous, why not invite fidget spinners back into the classroom with a new role as the spinner for a student-created game of Chutes and Ladders. All you need to get spinning are a protractor, ruler, piece of cardboard, some colored paper, and a glue gun.

RECYCLE THE ROTE TO CO-CREATE THE FUTURE

Most people would agree that there are certain foundational skills all citizens should acquire in their years of schooling. To the list of more traditional skills of literacy, numeracy, critical thinking, and problem solving are new skills such as identifying the most accurate information in a sea of falsehoods and navigating safely in a digital world. In order to learn these new skills, we'll need the communication and understanding grown from essential elements of numeracy and literacy that exist in our current curriculums. But what is not needed are the incessant worksheets, scripted curriculum, or partitioned content knowledge of decades gone by.

The expertise of educators lies in both teaching and observing our learners. Add this to the rich landscape of cognitive science that lies foundational to our work and we have a recipe for true innovation in education. Our opportunity, then, is based on harnessing our expertise to continually ask questions supported by cognitive science and continuously seek out novel ways to engage and enhance student learning. To do this we need to toss out the rote curriculum of yesteryear and usher in a future of learning in which together with our students we co-create the low-stakes but more applied and purposeful learning they will need today and in their future.

The most inspiring potential of play, to me, is that as educators we can build the future of play with our students today. We have all we need right in front of us. We have a solid understanding of how our students learn best and access to creative tools that can be used to create a global network of seekers and supporters in better understanding the world around us.

In fact, I would argue that the very best use of play has yet to even be played. And this is where you come in: cultivating the creators of the future right now in your classroom. One of the greatest challenges we face as a global community is how to communicate effectively to ensure all our diverse needs are met.

To engage in this work on such a large scale requires patience and reflection as well as the inherent iteration and persistence found in play. What do you care about, what do you want to solve, how can you use an existing game, tech, or tool to create an experience that helps you and your students tackle that issue? There is no limit to the ways in which we can use games and play to help our students learn and grow.

CONCLUSION: CHANGING THE GAME, FROM CONSUMPTION TO CREATION

I watch closely as my eleven-year-old son works to chain together code-blocks. He's just learned to use the pseudo-programming language in MinecraftEdu and is working hard to create and execute different commands. He's currently working furiously to build a machine that will deliver a sword at the push of a button.

As I watch quietly, I see that there are important components of different commands. For instance, you can use the command *give* to allow you to pass certain properties on to another player. But is it passed to a random player, the nearest player, the last one to enter the game? These are important distinctions! Then there's the object that you are trying to give to another. Are you passing along a sword or a block of wood? And finally, there are properties of the objects themselves. For instance, enchantments or sharpness must be considered when giving objects like swords.

To execute a specific command, a series of if-then statements must be strung together. These if-then (conditional) statements are complex but necessary to ensure the command is executed. This is no small feat. I ask questions while watching, which at first seems to irritate him but later he takes it in stride, checking his code and exhaling with relief when he adds the requisite redstone device and codes each successive command block, clicking *done* and activating the command.

An electrical engineer knows that if there is power, then something happens, whereas if there is no power, then nothing happens. While my son is not an electrical engineer (yet?), he is testing each conditional statement to activate command blocks using theories he'll learn later in geometry and drawing on understanding of simple machines from general science classes and perhaps later physics.

Within this experience, he's demonstrated an understanding of the structures of programming. This includes loops and if-then statements, as well as the fundamentals of objects and their attributes and properties. He's conducted tests of hypotheses by activating commands and emerged victorious in crafting a machine that, if you press a button, will reward you with a diamond sword.

Sure, no sooner had he completed this masterpiece than his brother came along and pressed the lever sixty-four times, acquiring sixty-four diamond swords. However, this led to his little brother becoming curious about how this magical item was crafted, leading him to wonder aloud, "Can we use codeblocks to enchant armor?" Immediately, my sons set off together to test their hypothesis and work to create a complete set of gear.

The Proof Is in the Playing

Early in life, long before we enter a geometry classroom, we learn about conditional statements. For instance: if I color on this wall in marker (hypothesis), then I am likely to get a talking to by Mom (conclusion).

We understand inherently that certain actions are likely to result in certain outcomes.

Perhaps this early understanding of conditional statements is also the beginning of deductive reasoning, an essential element of critical thinking. But our conceptual understanding of geometry is established long before we learn the term conditional statements. And the way in which we learn about the conditions of these statements is in the way we operate within our world, through play.

Whether dripping wet sand to make mud castles, placing Lego blocks atop one another together to build Batman's hideout, or crafting a sword in *Minecraft*, children are learning proofs. If the mud is too wet, then it will not hold the castle together. If the secret entrance to the Batcave is three bricks high, then the Batmobile will fit inside. If I place two diamonds and one stick in the correct pattern, then I will craft a diamond sword.

Sure, it's simpler than saying if triangles are congruent, then the triangle is a quadrilateral. But the concept is the same. In each instance, there are rules for testing whether or not the hypothesis will result in the anticipated conclusion. And the results of that test, or experiment, determines whether or not the conditional statement is correct.

So, I'm left to wonder why many students dislike geometry and love *Minecraft*, when they're learning similar concepts. What comes back as an answer time and again is that the world needs teachers who are guides on the side igniting our students' innate curiosity. Our job is to shepherd our students toward learning content in a way that it is understood conceptually and can be applied in the world around them.

Coding languages change every three years, conceptual understanding does not. So the code is not the point. Just like the game is not the point. It's not the game, it's the play. When kids are driven to create through play, their conceptual learning is rich, deep, and meaningful.

Not all play is equal to learning, but if we connect with our students while they are engaged in play, then we'll have a greater chance of seeing what matters to them and how they ultimately make sense of the world around them.

WHAT MATTERS MOST?

As educators we're suffering from whiplash as a result of ever-changing curricula mapped on to a revolving door of sanctions. Approaches to teaching and learning change faster than schools banned fidget spinners.

But why are we chasing fads and trying new tools instead of looking at our kids when they learn naturally: through play? Play is creation and so much more. Based on foundational skills such as literacy and numeracy, play helps essential understanding emerge through shared language, tools, and co-created experiences.

In these pages we've seen how the siloes of content and behavior, from social studies to social-emotional learning, can be woven together through play. And we've seen how this type of learning is more likely to enhance relationships, empower learners, and lead to sustained inquiry!

In Chapter 1 we learned how humans are hardwired to learn. Together we unpacked our neural circuitry to discover how humans grow and learn in ways that beautifully map onto game play. The way our brains grow and reorganize through myelination and pruning neurons not only helps us become more efficient learners but provides ample evidence for the "use it or lose it" rule of applying knowledge to secure learning. We discovered how games could be used to teach a variety of skills across contexts, including ways our students might design their own playful learning experiences!

The shared agreements that create parameters for our play are our rules. These rules were discussed in Chapter 2, where we saw how engaged and supportive collaborative communities ensure everyone has a role. Shared agreements give every player a voice in the creative process and are connected to social constructivist learning theories. We learned from research that making up rules to a game can be even more engaging than game play itself. We learned how multiple modalities of game play can be used to mirror real or fictional experiences across mediums to enhance and extend learning.

We discussed the theories of motivation driving each of our learners and how they take flight during play. In Chapter 3 we discussed important theories such as self-determination, where competence, autonomy, and relatedness give learners the key to their own CAR to drive learning. It became immediately clear how placing students at the wheel follows the best methods for student-centered learning and provides learners with countless opportunities to master higher-order skills like metacognition and self-regulation.

Iteration and reflection embedded in play helps players see themselves as a work in progress. In Chapter 4 we dug into the idea of failure as feedback and how games really teach our students how the pivots we take during play changes outcomes in games and in life. We talked about ways to use games to include rich and reflective self-feedback.

Embedded within the reflection and feedback learners receive during game play are important opportunities to use critical skills they will need to find success in the future. Chapter 5 discussed the way group dynamics support learning during game play, from collaboration and communication to strategic planning and empathy building. We learned how to use games to take the perspective of others and how that in turn plants the seeds of empathy.

The powerful formative feedback games and play provides to learners is an opportunity for educators to gain valuable insight into our students' experiences, to help them level up. In Chapter 6 we discovered that games often *are* the assessment. Learning about working memory and the power of repetition, rehearsal, and timing made it easy to see how ongoing feedback during game play may help grow dendrites!

Grounded in learning theory such as situated cognition, Chapter 7 shared the ways in which the roles students take on have the potential to impact them far beyond the four walls of your classroom. Together we mapped the nature of learning and explored some familiar and novel gaming experiences to discover how students might engage in more meaningful play to impact the world around them.

Learning content and behavior synchronously sends neurotransmitters to secure learning. And in these interdisciplinary and multimodal approaches to learning through play we're both deepening learning while making it fun. So why not use play to create foundational skills of literacy, numeracy, and critical thinking, and invite students to be designers and co-creators? Chapter 8 concludes with multiple opportunities to level up and invite students to get into the game (design)!

BONUS STAGE: CREATE, COMMUNICATE, CO-CREATE, CALIBRATE

The students in our classrooms today are the leaders of tomorrow's world. The exciting and complex futures they face are changing faster than ever before. But the regenerative and endless nature of play ensures our students can see themselves in the process of co-creating the future together. Driven by our students' curiosity and supported by expert educators, we can co-create the change we want to see in the world, beginning with the future we want each of our children to inhabit.

The process of play requires creation. But it also requires communication with others to be optimally successful. The skills baked into play help students connect to one another with a shared purpose. In defining the parameters of play, we grow content knowledge and develop a shared language, another powerful byproduct of play. And by placing the learning in the hands of our students, we are honoring their unique voices in learning each day.

It is in the calibration of learning through play that we see opportunities as educators to iterate, innovate, and inspire. If a lesson didn't go well last period, we likely won't repeat the same lesson to our next period of students. So beyond simply pleading for students to engage in playful learning, the hope here is that as the grown-ups in the space, you too will play alongside your learners!

Hélène Michel, professor of management and creativity at Grenoble École de Management in France, says that "being involved in a game gives you signals that you are protected in what you share."[79] By sharing more playful experiences, we're sending signals to our students that they are safe, that their voice matters, and that whatever is missing from today can always be made up again tomorrow. Imagine how powerful a classroom mantra like that could be for each child across the globe. We see you, we love you, and if you struggle, we're here to pick you up and help you try again tomorrow.

Empowered to be solutionaries instead of receptacles of rote worksheets, each of our students will greet the freedom to design the change they want to be in the world, demonstrating impressive learning and growth.

So What Are You Waiting For? Go Play!

In writing this book my goal was to take research from the ivory towers and make it readily applicable to classrooms today. The lived experiences I've shared alongside this research, as well as the examples of countless approaches to applying this learning, make it clear that our learning environments are ripe for some serious innovation.

The goal then is being inclusive in the way we invite more of our schools and more of our students to find the joy in learning through play. How will we address the current inequities so deeply entrenched in our public schools? How can we take our knowledge and use it to advocate for a different, better, and new way of doing school?

We've seen how our students come to the classroom not as checklists with a series of tasks or vessels we must fill while they're in our care but as endlessly imaginative and curious creatures whose cognitive architecture was built for tinkering and testing and refining together. The tools to unleash this magic are now within your reach. In fact, they've always been there, just waiting for you. They're sitting in your classroom each Monday morning, eager to see how you'll broach new subjects and waiting for an invitation to share in the magic of learning.

Together we've unpacked some of the cognitive science beneath learning and developed a shared language to show just how powerful playful experiences can be. Our task now is to work to foster these authentic learning experiences within our own classrooms intentionally, curating artifacts of awesomeness and documenting the progress of our learners. Together we can all design the change we want to see in education by bringing back the most impactful way we know to learn: play.

It's not the game, it's the play.

It's not the tool, it's the teacher.

The question now is not how to work more playful learning into each day, but rather, with so many choices and so little time, what games will you choose?

Scratch that, just go!

Time's a wastin': GO PLAY!

. . . and if you're feeling generous you can bring me along as well!

NOTES

1   Lillard, Angeline S. 2013. "Playful Learning and Montessori Education."
    NAMTA Journal 38, no. 2: 137–174.

2   Cincan, Alina. 2013, December 13. "Childhood Playground
    Games—A Multilingual Comparison of Etymology."
    Inbox Translation. https:// inboxtranslation.com/blog/
    childhood-playground-game s-multilingual-comparison-etymology/

3   Opie, Iona Archibald, and Peter Opie. 1969. *Children's Games in Street
    and Playground: Chasing, Catching, Seeking, Hunting, Racing, Duelling,
    Exerting, Daring, Guessing, Acting, Pretending.* Oxford: Clarendon Press.

4   Eisen, George. 1988. *Children and Play in the Holocaust: Games among the
    Shadows.* Amherst: University of Massachusetts Press.

5   Neill, Alexander Sutherland, and A. Summerhill. 1960. *A Radical
    Approach to Child Rearing.* New York: Hart.

6   Blair, Clancy. 2016. "Developmental Science and Executive Function."
    Current Directions in Psychological Science 25 (1): 3–7.

7   Karagiorgas, Dimitrios N., and Shari Niemann. 2017. "Gamification and
    Game-based Learning." *Journal of Educational Technology Systems* 45, no.
    4: 499–519.

8   Phillips, Deborah A., and Jack P. Shonkoff, eds. 2000. *From Neurons to
    Neighborhoods: The Science of Early Childhood Development.* Washington,
    DC: National Academies Press.

9   Salzer, J. L., and B. Zalc. 2016. "Myelination." *Current Biology* 26, no.
    20: R971–R975.

10 Begley, Sharon. 2007. *Train Your Mind, Change Your Brain: How a New
    Science Reveals Our Extraordinary Potential to Transform Ourselves.* New
    York: Random House Digital, Inc.

11 Wang, Song, Jing Dai, Jingguang Li, Xu Wang, Taolin Chen, Xun Yang,
    Manxi He, and Qiyong Gong. 2018. "Neuroanatomical Correlates of
    Grit: Growth Mindset Mediates the Association Between Gray Matter
    Structure and Trait Grit in Late Adolescence." *Human Brain Mapping* 39,
    no. 4: 1688–1699.

12 De Freitas, Sara. 2018. "Are Games Effective Learning Tools? A Review of
    Educational Games." *Journal of Educational Technology & Society* 21, no.
    2: 74–84.

13 Galván-Pérez, Laura, Tania Ouariachi, M. Pozo-Llorente, and José
    Gutiérrez-Pérez. 2018. "Outstanding Videogames on Water: A Quality
    Assessment Review Based on Evidence of Narrative, Gameplay and
    Educational Criteria." *Water* 10, no. 10: 1404.

14 Schrier, Karen. 2016. *Knowledge Games: How Playing Games Can Solve
    Problems, Create Insight, and Make Change.* Baltimore: Johns Hopkins
    University Press.

15 Schrier, Karen. 2019. *Learning, Education & Games, Volume 3: 100 Games to Use in the Classroom & Beyond*. Lulu.com.

16 Pesce, Caterina, Ilaria Masci, Rosalba Marchetti, Spyridoula Vazou, Arja Sääkslahti, and Phillip D. Tomporowski. 2016. "Deliberate Play and Preparation Jointly Benefit Motor and Cognitive Development: Mediated and Moderated Effects." *Frontiers in Psychology* 7: 349.

17 Diamond, Adele, and Kathleen Lee. 2011. "Interventions Shown to Aid Executive Function Development in Children 4 to 12 years old." *Science* 333, no. 6045: 959–964.

18 Fiske, Abigail, and Karla Holmboe. 2019. "Neural Substrates of Early Executive Function Development." *Developmental Review* 52: 42–62.

19 Fredericks, Claude R., Shirley J. Kokot, and Susan Krog. 2006. "Using a Developmental Movement Programme to Enhance Academic Skills in Grade 1 Learners." *South African Journal for Research in Sport, Physical Education and Recreation* 28, no. 1: 29–42.

20 Vygotsky, Lev S. 1967. "Play and Its Role in the Mental Development of the Child." *Soviet Psychology* 5, no. 3: 6–18.

21 Wallace, Claire E., and Sandra W. Russ. 2015. "Pretend Play, Divergent Thinking, and Math Achievement in Girls: A Longitudinal Study." *Psychology of Aesthetics, Creativity, and the Arts* 9, no. 3: 296–305.

22 Chayka, Kyle. August 6, 2016. "Same Old, Same Old: How the Hipster Aesthetic is Taking Over the World." *The Guardian* 7.

23 Piaget, Jean. 2003. "Part I: Cognitive–Piaget Development and Learning." *Journal of Research in Science Teaching* 40: S8–S18.

24 Bandura, Albert. 1982. "Self-Efficacy Mechanism in Human Agency." *American Psychologist* 37, no. 2: 122.

25 Siegel, Daniel J. 2002. *The Developing Mind: How Relationships and the Brain Interact to Shape Who We Are*. New York: Guilford Press.

26 Iacoboni, Marco, Istvan Molnar-Szakacs, Vittorio Gallese, Giovanni Buccino, John C. Mazziotta, and Giacomo Rizzolatti. 2005. "Grasping the Intentions of Others with One's Own Mirror Neuron System." *PLoS Biology* 3, no. 3: e79.

27 Carr, Laurie, Marco Iacoboni, Marie-Charlotte Dubeau, John C. Mazziotta, and Gian Luigi Lenzi. 2013. "Neural Mechanisms of Empathy in Humans: A Relay from Neural Systems for Imitation to Limbic Areas." *Proceedings of the National Academy of Sciences* 100, no. 9: 5497–5502.

28 Phillips, Deborah A., and Jack P. Shonkoff, eds. 2000. *From Neurons to Neighborhoods: The Science of Early Childhood Development*. Washington, DC: National Academies Press.

29 Portnoy, Lindsay. April 14, 2017. "Human Motivation in the Fourth Industrial Revolution." Digital Culturist. https://digitalculturist.com/human-motivation-in-the-fourth-industrial-revolution-78e82552030d.

30 Deci, Edward L., and Richard M. Ryan. 2008. "Self-Determination Theory: A Macrotheory of Human Motivation, Development, and Health." *Canadian Psychology/Psychologie Canadienne* 49, no. 3: 182–185.

31 Núñez, Juan L., and Jaime León. 2015. "Autonomy Support in the Classroom: *A Review from Self-Determination Theory.*" *European Psychologist* 20, no. 4: 275–283.

32 Ericsson, K. Anders. 2016. "Summing Up Hours of Any Type of Practice Versus Identifying Optimal Practice Activities: Commentary on Macnamara, Moreau, & Hambrick." *Perspectives on Psychological Science* 11, no. 3: 351–354.

33 Boot, Walter R., Anna Sumner, Tyler J. Towne, Paola Rodriguez, and K. Anders Ericsson. 2017. "Applying Aspects of the Expert Performance Approach to Better Understand the Structure of Skill and Mechanisms of Skill Acquisition in Video Games." *Topics in Cognitive Science* 9, no. 2: 413–436.

34 Vygotsky, Lev S. 1967. "Play and Its Role in the Mental Development of the Child." *Soviet Psychology* 5, no. 3: 6–18.

35 Ellison, Tisha Lewis, and Jessica N. Evans. 2016. "'Minecraft,' Teachers, Parents, and Learning: What They Need to Know and Understand." *School Community Journal* 26, no. 2: 25–43.

36 Shulman, Lee S. 2015. "PCK: Its Genesis and Exodus." In *Re-Examining Pedagogical Content Knowledge in Science Education*, edited by Amanda Berry, Patricia Friedrichsen, and John Loughran, 13–23. New York: Routledge.

37 Meier, Deborah. 2002. *In Schools We Trust: Creating Communities of Learning in an Era of Testing and Standardization.* Boston: Beacon Press.

38 Surma, Tim, Kristel Vanhoyweghen, Gino Camp, and Paul A. Kirschner. 2018. "The Coverage of Distributed Practice and Retrieval Practice in Flemish and Dutch Teacher Education Textbooks." *Teaching and Teacher Education* 74: 229–237.

39 Bandura, Albert. 2006. "Guide for Constructing Self-Efficacy Scales." *Self-Efficacy Beliefs of Adolescents* 5, no. 1, edited by Frank Pajares and Timothy C. Urdan, 307–337. Charlotte: Information Age Publishing.

40 Yoo, Hana, Xin Feng, and Randal D. Day. 2013. "Adolescents' Empathy and Prosocial Behavior in the Family Context: A Longitudinal Study." *Journal of Youth and Adolescence* 42, no. 12: 1858–1872.

41 Bandura, Albert, Dorothea Ross, and Sheila A. Ross. 1961. "Transmission of Aggression through Imitation of Aggressive Models." *The Journal of Abnormal and Social Psychology* 63, no. 3: 575–582.

42 Bandura, Albert. 1982. "Self-Efficacy Mechanism in Human Agency." *American Psychologist* 37, no. 2: 122.

43 Bandura, Albert. 2016. "50: The Power of Observational Learning through Social Modeling." In *Scientists Making a Difference: One Hundred Eminent Behavioral and Brain Scientists Talk About Their Most Important Contributions*, edited by Robert J. Sternberg, Susan T. Fiske, and Donald J. Foss, 235. Cambridge: Cambridge University Press.

44 Ehrlich, Brenna. 2010, November 28. "How to Make Your Music Video Go Viral: 10 Tips from Cee-Lo, OK Go & More." Mashable. https://mashable.com/2010/11/28/viral-music-video-how-to/.

45 Atkinson, Richard C., and Richard M. Shiffrin. 1971. "The Control of Short-Term Memory." *Scientific American* 225, no. 2: 82–91.

46 Ophir, Eyal, Clifford Nass, and Anthony D. Wagner. 2009. "Cognitive Control in Media Multitaskers." *Proceedings of the National Academy of Sciences* 106, no. 37: 15583–15587.

47 Miller, George A. 1956. "The Magical Number Seven, Plus or Minus Two: Some Limits on our Capacity for Processing Information." *Psychological Review* 63, no. 2: 81–97.

48 Wilmer, Henry H., Lauren E. Sherman, and Jason M. Chein. 2017. "Smartphones and Cognition: A Review of Research Exploring the Links Between Mobile Technology Habits and Cognitive Functioning." *Frontiers in Psychology* 8: 605.

49 Voelker, Pascale, Denise Piscopo, Aldis P. Weible, Gary Lynch, Mary K. Rothbart, Michael I. Posner, and Cristopher M. Niell. 2017. "How Changes in White Matter Might Underlie Improved Reaction Time Due to Practice." *Cognitive Neuroscience* 8, no. 2: 112–118.

50 Voelker, Pascale, Mary K. Rothbart, and Michael I. Posner. 2016. "A Polymorphism Related to Methylation Influences Attention during Performance of Speeded Skills." *AIMS Neuroscience* 3, no. 1: 40–55.

51 Agarwal, Pooja K., and Henry L. Roediger III. 2018. "Lessons for Learning: How Cognitive Psychology Informs Classroom Practice." *Phi Delta Kappan* 100, no. 4: 8–12.

52 Seabrook, Rachel, Gordon D.A. Brown, and Jonathan E. Solity. 2005. "Distributed and Massed Practice: From Laboratory to Classroom." *Applied Cognitive Psychology* 19, no. 1: 107–122.

53 Dempster, Frank N. 1987. "Effects of Variable Encoding and Spaced Presentations on Vocabulary Learning." *Journal of Educational Psychology* 79, no. 2: 162–170.

54 Smith, Troy A., and Daniel R. Kimball. 2010. "Learning from Feedback: Spacing and the Delay–Retention Effect." *Journal of Experimental Psychology: Learning, Memory, and Cognition* 36, no. 1: 80–95.

55 Gerbier, Emilie, and Thomas C. Toppino. 2015. "The Effect of Distributed Practice: Neuroscience, Cognition, and Education." *Trends in Neuroscience and Education* 4, no. 3: 49–59.

56 Seabrook, Rachel, Gordon D.A. Brown, and Jonathan E. Solity. 2005. "Distributed and Massed Practice: From Laboratory to Classroom." *Applied Cognitive Psychology* 19, no. 1: 107–122.

57 Svihla, Vanessa, Michael J. Wester, and Marcia C. Linn. 2018. "Distributed Practice in Classroom Inquiry Science Learning." *Learning: Research and Practice* 4, no. 2: 180–202.

58 Birnbaum, Monica S., Nate Kornell, Elizabeth Ligon Bjork, and Robert A. Bjork. 2013. "Why Interleaving Enhances Inductive Learning: The Roles of Discrimination and Retrieval." *Memory & Cognition* 41, no. 3: 392–402.

59 Rohrer, Doug, Robert F. Dedrick, and Sandra Stershic. 2015. "Interleaved Practice Improves Mathematics Learning." *Journal of Educational Psychology* 107, no. 3: 900–908.

60 Hays, Matthew Jensen, Nate Kornell, and Robert A. Bjork. 2013. "When and Why a Failed Test Potentiates the Effectiveness of Subsequent Study." *Journal of Experimental Psychology: Learning, Memory, and Cognition* 39, no. 1: 290–296.

61 Fyfe, Emily R., and Bethany Rittle-Johnson. 2016. "Feedback Both Helps and Hinders Learning: The Causal Role of Prior Knowledge." *Journal of Educational Psychology* 108, no. 1: 82–97.

62 Sweller, John, Jeroen J. G. Van Merrienboer, and Fred G. W. C. Paas. 1998. "Cognitive Architecture and Instructional Design." *Educational Psychology Review* 10, no. 3: 251–296.

63 Van Popta, Esther, Marijke Kral, Gino Camp, Rob L. Martens, and P. Robert-Jan Simons. 2017. "Exploring the Value of Peer Feedback in Online Learning for the Provider." *Educational Research Review* 20: 24–34.

64 Kral, Tammi R. A., Diane E. Stodola, Rasmus M. Birn, Jeanette A. Mumford, Enrique Solis, Lisa Flook, Elena G. Patsenko, Craig G. Anderson, Constance Steinkuehler, and Richard J. Davidson. 2018. "Neural Correlates of Video Game Empathy Training in Adolescents: A Randomized Trial." *npj Science of Learning* 3, no. 1: 1–10.

65 Pilon, Mary. September 1, 2018. "Monopoly's Lost Female Inventor." National Women's History Museum. https://www.womenshistory. org/articles/monopolys-lost-female-inventor.

66 Crowley, Kevin, Maureen A. Callanan, Harriet R. Tenenbaum, and Elizabeth Allen. 2001. "Parents Explain More Often to Boys than to Girls during Shared Scientific Thinking." *Psychological Science* 12, no. 3: 258–261.

67 Passarelli, Angela M., and David A. Kolb. 2012. "Using Experiential Learning Theory to Promote Student Learning and Development in Programs of Education Abroad." In *Student Learning Abroad: What Our Students are Learning, What They're Not, and What We Can Do About It*, edited by Michael Vande Berg, Michael Page, and Chris Lou, 137–161. Sterling, VA: Stylus Publishing.

68 Brown, John Seely, Allan Collins, and Paul Duguid. 1989. "Situated Cognition and the Culture of Learning." *Educational Researcher* 18, no. 1: 32–42.

69 Kuhlthau, Carol Collier. 2009. "Guided Inquiry: Learning in the 21st Century." In *International Association of School Librarianship. Selected Papers from the . . . Annual Conference, International Association of School Librarianship*: 1.

70 Loehr, Abbey Marie, Emily R. Fyfe, and Bethany Rittle-Johnson. 2014. "Wait for It . . . Delaying Instruction Improves Mathematics Problem Solving: A Classroom Study." *The Journal of Problem Solving* 7, no. 1: 5.

71 Wall, Emily, Leslie M. Blaha, Celeste Lyn Paul, Kristin Cook, and Alex Endert. 2018. "Four Perspectives on Human Bias in Visual Analytics." In *Cognitive Biases in Visualizations*, edited by Geoffrey Ells, 29–42. Cham, Switzerland: Springer, Cham.

72 Hatfield, Bridget E. 2019. "The Influence of Teacher–Child Relationships on Preschool Children's Cortisol Levels." In *Biobehavioral Markers in Risk and Resilience Research*, edited by Amanda W. Harrist and Brandt C. Gardner, 69–89. Cham: Springer.

73 Felitti, Vincent J., Robert F. Anda, Dale Nordenberg, David F. Williamson, Alison M. Spitz, Valerie Edwards, Mary P. Koss, and James S. Marks. 2019. "Relationship of Childhood Abuse and Household Dysfunction to Many of the Leading Causes of Death in Adults: The Adverse Childhood Experiences (ACE) Study." *American Journal of Preventive Medicine* 56, no. 6: 774–786.

74 Hogue, Candace M., Mary D. Fry, and Andrew C. Fry. 2019. "The Protective Impact of Learning to Juggle in a Caring, Task-involving Climate versus an Ego-Involving Climate on Participants' Inflammation, Cortisol, and Psychological Responses." *International Journal of Sport and Exercise Psychology*: 1–18.

75 Eshel, Yohanan, and Revital Kohavi. 2003. "Perceived Classroom Control, Self-Regulated Learning Strategies, and Academic Achievement." *Educational Psychology* 23, no. 3: 249–260.

76 Portnoy, Lindsay. 2019. *Designed to Learn: Using Design Thinking to Bring Purpose and Passion to the Classroom*. Alexandria, VA: ASCD.

77 Denning, Tamara, Adam Lerner, Adam Shostack, and Tadayoshi Kohno. 2013. "Control-Alt-Hack: The Design and Evaluation of a Card Game for Computer Security Awareness and Education." In *Proceedings of the 2013 ACM SIGSAC Conference on Computer & Communications Security*, 915–928. ACM.

78 Eterna. August 29, 2017. "The Science and Puzzles of OpenCRISPR" [Video]. https://youtu.be/IGYpu4BVnhA.

79 Moules, Jonathan. December 1, 2019. "To the Escape Room! How Business Schools are Embracing Games." *Financial Times*. https://www.ft.com/content/106483a0-d3da-11e9-8367-807ebd53ab77.

ACKNOWLEDGMENTS

Thank you to the entire DBC family, whose cooperative play made the book in your hands a reality. From the moment we pressed play it was game on! My first conversations with Dave and Shelley were infused with possibility, and each successive team member really helped level up this book.

I am indebted to the insightful and patient Marisol Quevedo Rerucha for bringing a lens of equity to this work, and to the incredible work of Lindsey Alexander, Theresa Dowell Blackinton, Sophia Dembling, and Michael Miller who fine-tuned the beta version of this manuscript into a book ready for live release. To my fellow traveler, Tara Martin, thank you for your words of wisdom that inspire so many each day.

Many thanks to the educators who shared stories within these pages, and to the countless educators who gain maximum XP by bringing joy, inquiry, and excitement to their learners through play.

Playing *Super Mario Bros.* in my basement in 1984, I had no way of knowing that I'd set out on a lifelong journey to unlock more powerful learning through play. And yet it makes perfect sense each time I watch my children delight in the discovery of a hidden Easter egg that reveals an entirely new way to play.

Parenting isn't always a multiplayer game, which is why I'm grateful that I have a squad to help power up on the days when I fall from the leaderboard. Thank you to my husband, Gary, my parents and family, and all our dear friends, who upgrade our lives and generously entertain our constant shenanigans.

Thank you most of all to my epic sons, Judah and Levi, who never let me forget that "boomers" are "noobs" and that the true warp zone to engaged learning is always through play.

ABOUT THE AUTHOR

DR. LINDSAY PORTNOY is a cognitive scientist and associate teaching professor at Northeastern University, where she teaches doctoral courses within the graduate school of education. Portnoy is a former public-school teacher, cofounder of the immersive science learning company Killer Snails and has nearly two decades of experience in the study and instruction of cognition, human development, and assessment of teaching and learning from birth through adolescence. She has worked with thousands of educators and students across the globe in both formal and informal settings including the American Museum of Natural History, the New York Botanical Garden and the New York Hall of Science, where she facilitates workshops and delivers professional development and keynotes.

Dr. Portnoy is a former ASCD Emerging Leader and Assessment Fellow at Hunter College, CUNY. She is a member of the World Economic Forum's Expert Network in Media, Entertainment. Portnoy writes and researches at the intersection of cognition, assessment for learning, and emerging technology, and her work has been published in peer-reviewed journals including the *Journal for Accessibility, Compliance, & Equity,* the *Journal of Games, Society, and Self,* and the *Journal of Educational Research and Assessment* as well as in such widely read publications as the *Washington Post, USA Today,* The 74, EdSurge, the World Economic Forum, Getting Smart, ASCD, The Age of Awareness, and Digital Culturist. Her book *Designed to Learn: Using Design Thinking to Bring Purpose and Passion to the Classroom* was published by ASCD in November of 2019.

READY TO LEVEL UP EVEN MORE? GAME ON!

These keynotes, talks, and workshops are rooted in cognitive science and honor voices of all stakeholders around topics including the future of learning, art of assessment, science of play, power of design thinking, and secrets to empowering all stakeholders in sustainable change:

THE FUTURE OF EDUCATION AND INNOVATION:
- **KEYNOTE:** Designing a More Equitable Educational Future
- **TALK:** Igniting Innovation in Local and Global Education
- **WORKSHOP:** Solving the Problems of Tomorrow with the Learners of Today

THE ART OF FORMATIVE ASSESSMENT:
- **KEYNOTE:** Demystifying Assessment: Formative Practices to Level Up Assessment in Every Classroom
- **TALK:** Deepening Engagement Through the Intentional Application of Emerging Technologies
- **WORKSHOP:** Level Up Your Assessment Practices: Calibrating Assessment Through Communities of Practice

THE SCIENCE OF PLAY:
- **KEYNOTE:** Bugatti and the Brain: The Striking Similarity Between Play & Gray (Matter)
- **TALK:** Designed to Play! Creating Playful Learning in Every Classroom from K-Gray
- **WORKSHOP:** More than a Score: How Play Levels Up Learning

THE POWER OF DESIGN THINKING:
- **KEYNOTE:** Designed to Learn: Using Design Thinking to Bring Purpose and Passion to the Classroom
- **TALK:** Paper to Plan: A Protocol for Co-Creating the Change We Want to Be in the World
- **WORKSHOP:** 0-60: Design Thinking to Create an MVP

THE SECRETS TO EMPOWERING ALL STAKEHOLDERS IN A LOCAL AND GLOBAL LEARNING COMMUNITY:

- **KEYNOTE:** Better Together: Maintaining the Sustainability of the Joy of Teaching
- **TALK:** Raising Community Voice to Design the Change We Want to Be in the World
- **WORKSHOP:** Team Building: Raising Voices of All Stakeholders to Create a Shared Vision

MORE FROM

DAVE BURGESS
Consulting, Inc.

Since 2012, DBCI has been publishing books that inspire and equip educators to be their best. For more information on our titles or to purchase bulk orders for your school, district, or book study, visit **DaveBurgessconsulting.com/DBCIbooks**.

MORE INSPIRATION, PROFESSIONAL GROWTH & PERSONAL DEVELOPMENT

Be REAL by Tara Martin

Be the One for Kids by Ryan Sheehy

The Coach ADVenture by Amy Illingworth

Creatively Productive by Lisa Johnson

Educational Eye Exam by Alicia Ray

The EduNinja Mindset by Jennifer Burdis

Empower Our Girls by Lynmara Colón and Adam Welcome

Finding Lifelines by Andrew Grieve and Andrew Sharos

The Four O'Clock Faculty by Rich Czyz

How Much Water Do We Have? by Pete and Kris Nunweiler

If the Dance Floor is Empty, Change the Song by Dr. Joe Clark

P Is for Pirate by Dave and Shelley Burgess

A Passion for Kindness by Tamara Letter

The Path to Serendipity by Allyson Apsey

Sanctuaries by Dan Tricarico

The SECRET SAUCE by Rich Czyz

Shattering the Perfect Teacher Myth by Aaron Hogan

Stories from Webb by Todd Nesloney

Talk to Me by Kim Bearden
Teach Better by Chad Ostrowski, Tiffany Ott, Rae Hughart, and Jeff Gargas
Teach Me, Teacher by Jacob Chastain
Teach, Play, Learn! by Adam Peterson
TeamMakers by Laura Robb and Evan Robb
Through the Lens of Serendipity by Allyson Apsey
The Zen Teacher by Dan Tricarico

LIKE A PIRATE™ SERIES

Teach Like a PIRATE by Dave Burgess
eXPlore Like a Pirate by Michael Matera
Learn Like a Pirate by Paul Solarz
Play Like a Pirate by Quinn Rollins
Run Like a Pirate by Adam Welcome
Tech Like a PIRATE by Matt Miller

LEAD LIKE A PIRATE™ SERIES

Lead Like a PIRATE by Shelley Burgess and Beth Houf
Balance Like a Pirate by Jessica Cabeen, Jessica Johnson, and Sarah Johnson
Lead beyond Your Title by Nili Bartley
Lead with Appreciation by Amber Teamann and Melinda Miller
Lead with Culture by Jay Billy
Lead with Instructional Rounds by Vicki Wilson
Lead with Literacy by Mandy Ellis

LEADERSHIP & SCHOOL CULTURE

Culturize by Jimmy Casas
Escaping the School Leader's Dunk Tank by Rebecca Coda and Rick Jetter
From Teacher to Leader by Starr Sackstein
The Innovator's Mindset by George Couros

It's OK to Say "They" by Christy Whittlesey
Kids Deserve It! by Todd Nesloney and Adam Welcome
Live Your Excellence by Jimmy Casas
Let Them Speak by Rebecca Coda and Rick Jetter
The Limitless School by Abe Hege and Adam Dovico
Next-Level Teaching by Jonathan Alsheimer
The Pepper Effect by Sean Gaillard
The Principled Principal by Jeffrey Zoul and Anthony McConnell
Relentless by Hamish Brewer
The Secret Solution by Todd Whitaker, Sam Miller, and
    Ryan Donlan
Start. Right. Now. by Todd Whitaker, Jeffrey Zoul, and Jimmy Casas
Stop. Right. Now. by Jimmy Casas and Jeffrey Zoul
Teach Your Class Off by CJ Reynolds
They Call Me "Mr. De" by Frank DeAngelis
Unmapped Potential by Julie Hasson and Missy Lennard
Word Shift by Joy Kirr
Your School Rocks by Ryan McLane and Eric Lowe

TECHNOLOGY & TOOLS

50 Things You Can Do with Google Classroom by Alice Keeler
    and Libbi Miller
50 Things to Go Further with Google Classroom by Alice Keeler
    and Libbi Miller
140 Twitter Tips for Educators by Brad Currie, Billy Krakower,
    and Scott Rocco
Block Breaker by Brian Aspinall
Code Breaker by Brian Aspinall
Control Alt Achieve by Eric Curts
Google Apps for Littles by Christine Pinto and Alice Keeler
Master the Media by Julie Smith
Reality Bytes by Christine Lion-Bailey, Jesse Lubinsky, and
    Micah Shippee, PhD

Sail the 7 Cs with Microsoft Education by Becky Keene
  and Kathi Kersznowski

Shake Up Learning by Kasey Bell

Social LEADia by Jennifer Casa-Todd

Stepping Up to Google Classroom by Alice Keeler and
  Kimberly Mattina

Teaching Math with Google Apps by Alice Keeler and
  Diana Herrington

Teachingland by Amanda Fox and Mary Ellen Weeks

TEACHING METHODS & MATERIALS

All 4s and 5s by Andrew Sharos

Boredom Busters by Katie Powell

The Classroom Chef by John Stevens and Matt Vaudrey

The Collaborative Classroom by Trevor Muir

Copyrighteous by Diana Gill

Ditch That Homework by Matt Miller and Alice Keeler

Ditch That Textbook by Matt Miller

Don't Ditch That Tech by Matt Miller, Nate Ridgway, and
  Angelia Ridgway

EDrenaline Rush by John Meehan

Educated by Design by Michael Cohen, The Tech Rabbi

The EduProtocol Field Guide by Marlena Hebern and Jon Corippo

The EduProtocol Field Guide: Book 2 by Marlena Hebern and
  Jon Corippo

Instant Relevance by Denis Sheeran

LAUNCH by John Spencer and A. J. Juliani

Make Learning MAGICAL by Tisha Richmond

Pure Genius by Don Wettrick

The Revolution by Darren Ellwein and Derek McCoy

Shift This! by Joy Kirr

Skyrocket Your Teacher Coaching by Michael Cary Sonbert

Spark Learning by Ramsey Musallam

Sparks in the Dark by Travis Crowder and Todd Nesloney

Table Talk Math by John Stevens

The Wild Card by Hope and Wade King

The Writing on the Classroom Wall by Steve Wyborney

CHILDREN'S BOOKS

Beyond Us by Aaron Polansky

Cannonball In by Tara Martin

Dolphins in Trees by Aaron Polansky

I Want to Be a Lot by Ashley Savage

The Princes of Serendip by Allyson Apsey

The Wild Card Kids by Hope and Wade King

Zom-Be a Design Thinker by Amanda Fox

Made in the USA
Columbia, SC
11 January 2023

10067155R10096